Flourish
After Fifty

A SELF-LOVE WORKBOOK FOR WOMEN

FIRESIDE
PUBLISHING GROUP
TELL YOUR STORY ● IGNITE CHANGE

Copyright 2025

Fireside Publishing Group

ISBN: 979-8-9916617-0-6 Paperback

ISBN: 979-8-9916617-1-3 eBook

ISBN: 979-8-9916617-2-0 Audio

Fireside Publishing Group
Fayetteville, AR 72756

Printed in the USA

Disclaimer

The content in Flourish After Fifty: A Self-Love Workbook for Women is only intended for informational and inspirational purposes. The author does not hold a license as a mental healthcare professional and draws on a collection of methods and processes she found instrumental in transformation and personal development for the exercises and guidance in the book.

Personal growth is a unique and individual experience, and as such, this book cannot guarantee specific results. If you are experiencing emotional distress or mental health challenges or require personalized support, the reader is encouraged to seek assistance from a licensed healthcare professional.

Table of Contents

"Self-love is not about being self-centered; it's about being centered in yourself."

– Lalah Delia

Introduction

Instead of a midlife crisis, experience a midlife transformation. Rather than falling apart or fading into the background, midlife is the perfect time to step into your power and shine. This season of life invites you to pause, reflect, and realign with what truly matters—shedding the expectations and roles that no longer fit. Perfection doesn't need to be chased, and nothing about you needs fixing. Instead, reclaim the peace, wisdom, and confidence already inside you. Midlife isn't the beginning of the end—it's a major intersection where you get to rewrite the next chapter and bring new meaning to the golden years ahead. Yes, life will happen, but loving yourself enough to reclaim your authenticity and realign with what matters in this stage of life is revolutionary.

Who's with me?

AN EPIPHANY IN STILLNESS

One day, during meditation, feeling drained from constantly trying to do and achieve more, I decided to jump off the proverbial treadmill and stop pushing myself to become more. In that moment of surrender, I experienced an epiphany—an awareness like never before. The dialogue in my head went like this — *"stop becoming the best version of yourself. Be the best version of yourself in this moment. You already have everything you need. 'Becoming' means you believe you're not good enough yet. It means you don't accept yourself. You see yourself as flawed. Unconditionally love and accept yourself exactly as you are right now."*

With my eyes still closed, one undeniable truth blossomed, a knowing so deep it transcended anything I'd felt or understood before. It was more than just an intellectual realization or an emotional release. It was a confident knowing. What I felt in my body matched the clarity in my mind. It flooded me with a sense of light and freedom paired with an undeniable clarity that resonated to my core. At that moment, everything made sense. I was grateful for my entire life, every hardship and every joy because it all led me here. I no longer needed to strive for worthiness or chase perfection.

A declaration formed in my mind: no more putting off happiness. No more, *"I'll be the best version of myself when I lose thirty pounds," "when I stop snapping at my kids,"* or *"when I get that promotion at work."* Then my breath slowed, and a calm fell over me—Aaaaahhhh, peace as I accepted the unedited truth about myself; I am enough simply because I exist.

LIBERATION DAY

Humans spend a lot of time chasing after peace, love, and happiness, thinking it's out there somewhere, waiting for us. News flash—it's not. It's already inside us, quietly waiting for us to stop, breathe, and notice. Intellectually, I knew happiness was something *"I am,"* not something I find. Yet, I lived for decades with subconscious beliefs driving socially acceptable behaviors that painted a different picture.

The honest answer to "Who am I?" has nothing to do with your job title, family roles, occupation, or the labels you've adopted. Dr. Wayne Dyer said it best: "You are not a human being having a spiritual experience. You are a spiritual being having a human experience."

The person you were at birth, the real you—the one who existed before the world told you who you should be—is still there, waiting to be rediscovered. And guess what? She has everything she needs to have the life she dreams of. She doesn't need fixing, perfecting, or permission to shine. In that meditation, I experienced radical self-acceptance or unconditional love for myself. When you realize, at a fundamental level, that there is nothing wrong with you, this acceptance creates a paradigm shift where you feel grateful for your entire life: the good, the bad, and the ugly. You accept that everything in your life transpired for your growth and ultimate good. That doesn't mean your experiences were easy. They will teach you to unearth your inner beauty and discover where your subconscious stores unhealthy fears, beliefs, and unprocessed emotions.

THE ADVENTURE

This book is your roadmap to rediscovering the incredible woman you've always been—the one who exists beneath the layers of stress, societal expectations, and self-doubt. It's time to put yourself at the top of your to-do list and embark on a transformative path of self-awareness guided by the wisdom already inside you. Here's what you'll find:

Flourishing begins with self-love. When you release the fear of judgment and stop chasing external validation, you create space to reconnect with your desires, values, and authenticity. By peeling back the layers of ego and limiting beliefs, you uncover the vibrant soul beneath—the part of you that is always enough.

Explore your shadow side—the hidden fears, childhood stories, and unprocessed emotions that hold you back. Instead of avoiding these parts of yourself, you'll learn to meet them with compassion and curiosity, turning them from obstacles into stepping stones for growth.

Recognize your energy drains. Society not only accepts but celebrates certain behaviors—busyness, people-pleasing, constant striving for perfection—all in the name of "success" or "being a good person." These behaviors might earn praise from others, but they come at a cost—our energy, authenticity, and peace of mind. Social norms often encourage us to shrink ourselves to fit roles. These patterns don't serve us; they keep us small.

Conquer the setbacks that leave you in pieces. True transformation happens when you allow life's setbacks to become testaments of resilience and beauty. By embracing forgiveness, gratitude, and vulnerability, you'll see the value in every experience—good, bad, or messy. With these tools, you'll learn to let go of what no longer serves you, reclaim your energy, and step into the fullness of your power.

This book is packed with information and exercises to help you live with intention and authenticity. As you reconnect with your inner child, and tap into your soul's purpose, you'll build a life rooted in love, confidence, and abundance. No longer defined by fear or scarcity, you'll live as the most radiant, unapologetically real version of yourself.

Practical tools, reflective exercises, and mindful practices serve as personal coaching sessions, guiding you to apply what you've learned in real-time. You'll journal, reflect, and take small, manageable steps toward healing and transformation.

So, pour yourself a cup of coffee, a glass of wine, or whatever makes you feel cozy, and get ready for an adventure that will transform the way you see yourself and your life. It's time to stop chasing your dream and start living it.

Common Terms Defined

Before we dive in, let's get on the same page—literally. This glossary is parked right up front so you don't have to play hide-and-seek with unfamiliar terms later. Skim it, savor it, or ignore it entirely and live dangerously—it's your call. But if you stumble across a word later and think, "Wait, what does that mean again?"—well, don't say I didn't try to help.

Awareness – Awareness cultivates understanding and allows you to take a third-party view of your life. It heightens your understanding of how your environment, relationships, and inner narratives influence your life.

Boundaries – Setting boundaries is a transformative act of self-respect, enabling you to protect your time, energy, and emotional well-being.

Conscious Observer – The conscious observer is the aspect of your awareness that witnesses your thoughts, emotions, and experiences without judgment or attachment. It is the unchanging essence of you—the quiet presence that notices the chatter of the mind, the ebb and flow of emotions, and the unfolding of life's moments.

Core Values – Core values reconnect you with what truly matters to you, guiding your decisions and actions in alignment with your purpose.

Ego – The ego is the part of you that shapes your sense of identity and self-worth, often based on external achievements, beliefs, and societal expectations. It is the "I" or "me" that identifies with your thoughts, feelings, body, possessions, and roles in life.

Emotional Intelligence (EI) – Developing a healthy EI deepens your ability to understand, manage, and communicate your emotions while also empathizing with others. By strengthening this skill, you gain insight into the ways old thought patterns influence your reactions.

Inner GPS - Your Inner GPS is your built-in Genuine Path to Self, a navigation system for life. It aligns with your soul's purpose and core values.

Mindfulness – Mindfulness grounds you in the present moment, helping you tune into your thoughts, feelings, and physical sensations with curiosity and acceptance.

Self-love – Loving yourself is the conscious act of valuing and caring for yourself in a way that nurtures your true essence rather than feeding the ego's need for validation, control, or superiority. Self-love in this book refers to a love for the self that comes from a place of infinite power and balance, where you respect yourself while also honoring the interconnectedness of all relationships.

Soul – The soul is the timeless, boundless essence of who you truly are—the core of your being that transcends your physical body, personality, and the roles you play in the world. It is often described as the spark of divine energy, consciousness, or life force within you, representing your truest self and your connection to something greater.

The Shadow – The shadow refers to the hidden, often unconscious parts of yourself that you may suppress, deny, or reject because they conflict with your self-image or societal expectations. These aspects can include repressed emotions, fears, desires, or behaviors you deem unacceptable.

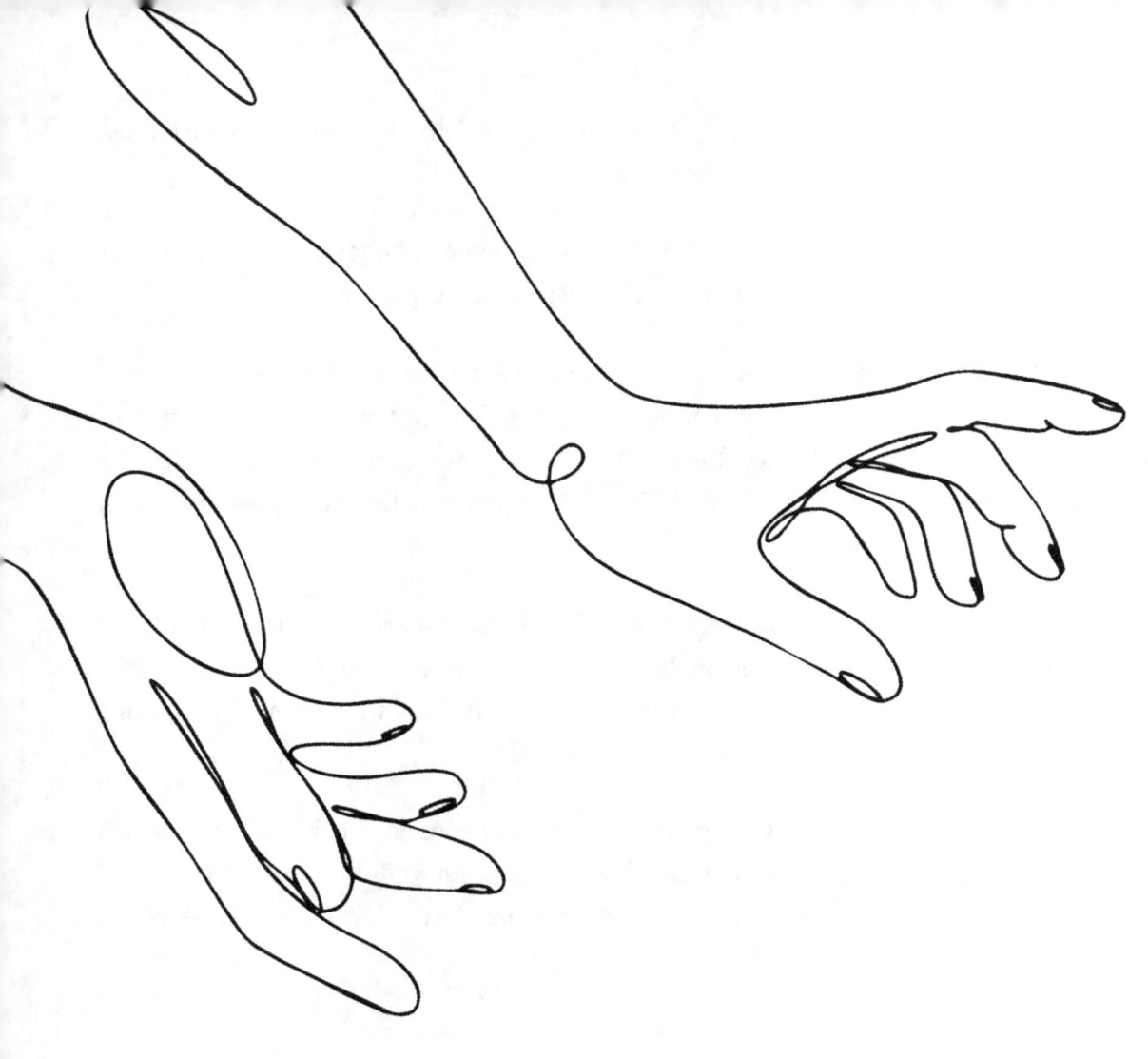

"You were wild once; don't let them tame you."

- Isadora Duncan

CHAPTER ONE

Love Yourself, Don't Lose Yourself

S elf-love is not the same as selfishness. I know, I know—some people might give you the side-eye and mutter something about 'me time' being all about ego. But that's not the case. Unlike the 'me first,' 'everyone do your own thing' selfish rebellion of the 1960s and 1970s, today's self-love movement is all about understanding your intrinsic value, nurturing your well-being, and making choices that genuinely support a healthy life.

When the ego is in charge, it's all about scarcity and fear. Selfishness comes from a place of fear— fear that there's not enough to go around, fear you'll miss out, fear that you're not good enough or smart enough. Like a toddler in a toy store demanding attention, the ego craves constant validation. And the irony? The more selfishly you act, the more disconnected you feel. You are taking something from others to fill your needs which repels people. Trying to meet your needs from external sources will inevitably fail because you see yourself lacking.

UNDERSTANDING MY LUXURY RADAR

Let me take you on a little trip down my self-love path. For as long as I can remember, every time I walked into a store, I made a beeline for the most expensive thing in the place (and still do). I have some kind of built-in luxury radar. In the past, I would judge myself pretty harshly for being attracted to expensive things. The erratic thoughts that went through my head sounded something like this..... *"You always pick out the most expensive thing in the store. Why are you so high maintenance?"* *"You can't afford that!"*

Even when I didn't buy anything, my mind spiraled out of control down the path of lack and comparison..... *"Why can't I make enough money to buy the things I want? Other people make money with ease."* —all classic ego propaganda. The feeling of lack would go into hyperdrive. My ego generated evidence in my life that I didn't value myself.

As I began practicing self-love, I noticed awareness, compassion, and acceptance were daily tools. These tools helped me shine a light into the shadows of my mind and discover the truth about myself. I began to honor what was important to me instead of living in the mindset of what I should or shouldn't want—realizing I wasn't selfish or materialistic, just discerning. Appreciating beauty is a quality, not a curse.

I discovered there is nothing wrong with valuing beauty and spotting high-quality, well-made things. My love for creating a visually appealing home, giving beautiful handmade gifts, or wearing nice clothes wasn't ego-driven. I wasn't trying to impress the neighbors or design an unaffordable lifestyle. I was just as happy buying cashmere sweaters from Goodwill as I was buying them from boutique stores. High price tags and designer labels didn't drive my motivation, nor did external praise. My motivation came from appreciating and wanting to share beauty. Aligning with my soul and identifying my core values rather than judging or suppressing them set me on a new path to discovering myself. So, instead of seeing my tastes as flaws, I accepted them as reflections of my true self.

Self-Love Inventory Exercise

Step 1: Self-love starts with self-awareness. Before you can fully step into self-love, it helps to get clear on what it means to you and why it matters. This exercise will give you a starting point—a personal roadmap to understanding your motivations, values, and intentions.

Answer the following.....

What's driving you to practice self-love? Why did you buy this book?

What do you think is meant by self-love?

What does it look like? Do you know a person you think has it?

What do you want to walk away with by completing this workbook?

Step 2: Create a snapshot of where you are in your self-love journey right now in four categories: heart, mind, body, and soul. For each statement below, rate yourself by using a number between 1-5. With 1 meaning rarely and 5 meaning most of the time.

Spiritual Well-Being

1. I trust that life is happening 'for' me, not 'to' me, even when things don't go as planned.

2. I recognize and release the belief that I need to be perfect to feel worthy.

3. I find peace in surrendering control and allowing life to unfold without trying to manage every detail.

4. I embrace uncertainty without needing constant reassurance or guarantees.

5. I recognize that I am not defined by my past, and I am free to create a new future based on unlimited abundance.

6. I embrace taking risks and stepping out of my comfort zone.

Mental Well-Being

1. I regularly challenge the beliefs I hold about who I 'should' be, and instead explore who I truly am.

2. I notice when my mind operates from fear or scarcity, and I consciously shift to a mindset of abundance and trust.

3. I can release old narratives about limits for me and allow myself to dream without restrictions.

4. I observe my limiting thoughts and patterns as temporary, rather than identifying with them.

5. I appreciate and enjoy my alone time.

6. I can easily name five things I like about myself.

7. I refrain from speaking negatively to myself.

8. I talk to myself with the same kindness and respect I would show to a best friend, partner, or child.

9. I am confident in making decisions, even if others disagree with me.

11. I feel at ease doing activities alone, such as going to a movie or dining out by myself.

Emotional Well-Being

1. I recognize that my emotional reactions are often rooted in past conditioning, and I respond with compassion rather than judgment.

2. I question whether difficult emotions are based on reality or old fears, rather than accepting them as truth.

3. I view my emotional vulnerability as a strength, rather than something to hide or protect.

4. I understand that feelings of unworthiness or lack are just stories I've learned, not my truth.

5. I feel complete and worthy within myself, regardless of external validation or others' opinions.

6. I acknowledge that my feelings are valid.

7. I recognize that my needs and desires are as important as those of others.

8. I am capable of making requests and asking for what I need without guilt.

9. I am comfortable with others disagreeing with me.

Physical Well-Being

1. I listen to my body's needs without judgment and honor what it asks for, whether it's rest, movement, or nourishment.

2. I engage in physical activity from a place of love and appreciation for my body, not from a place of lack or insecurity.

3. I let go of rigid expectations around food and exercise, trusting my body to guide me toward what is good for me.

4. I rest and rejuvenate my body without feeling guilty, knowing that rest is a necessary part of my well-being.

5. I accept and embrace my unique body, free from societal or personal pressures about how I 'should' look.

6. I prioritize exercising several times a week.

7. I choose foods that nourish my body.

Step 3: Take a moment to reflect on your Step 2 responses. Then answer the following questions:

Do you wish some of the statements could have a higher rating on the 1-5 scale? Which ones?

What parts of your life have the highest ratings and are in alignment with your authentic self?

Can you see in your ratings the grip of old narratives or beliefs that are no longer serving you? Make some preliminary notes.

What areas of your life need more compassion, self-acceptance, or freedom?

This evaluation is not meant to judge or criticize but to gently shine a light on where you might still be carrying subconscious beliefs that limit your potential. True freedom lies in understanding that you are not your mind, not your past, and not your limiting beliefs. Love is your natural state, and through the process of self-reflection, you can return to that innate origin.

Step 4: Set some intentional goals. Based on your answers to the previous question, create your personal goals. They can be big picture goals or daily goals. They need to be personal, meaningful, and, most importantly, achievable.

Permission Slip

What is something you're hesitant to embrace or fully enjoy due to your own judgement? Write yourself a permission slip to unapologetically embrace your authentic tastes and desires.

Example:

I give myself permission to appreciate _____without guilt.

How might embracing this desire benefit you?

THE HOARDING MENTALITY

When we're acting from a place of selfishness, our focus narrows. We become overly concerned with our needs and wants, often without considering the impact on those around us. This isolationist mindset cuts us off from genuine connection. It's an ego-based habit, a defense mechanism built on the idea that life is a zero-sum game. It perpetuates a sense of hoarding, not just material things but attention, recognition, and validation. Selfishness thrives on separateness. While hoarding may give a temporary sense of control or satisfaction, the irony is that selfishness leaves us feeling more disconnected from ourselves and those around us.

For example, think of someone constantly seeking praise or external validation to feel valuable. This person may perform acts of kindness, but their actions are often conditional—done with the expectation of receiving something in return, whether it be recognition, praise, or some other form of validation. This person operates from a sense of emptiness, needing people or things to fill the void because they are fractured and separated from the soul. Over time, hoarding behavior drives a wedge between them and others because it feels transactional, inauthentic, and ultimately exhausting for everyone involved.

Identify Limiting Beliefs

Step 1: Write down a belief or thought that makes you hesitate to prioritize yourself. Ask yourself, Is this belief rooted in fear or scarcity?

For example: *"If I spend time on myself, I'll neglect my responsibilities."*

Step 2: Now reframe the thought by rewriting the belief with a perspective of abundance.

For example: *"Taking time for myself allows me to show up more fully and lovingly for others."*

Step 3: Next, choose one small intentional act of self-care this week. Observe how it feels in the moment and how it affects your interactions with others.

Abundance Mindset List

Step 1: List Five ways you already experience abundance in your life—love, opportunities, support, comfort.

Step 2: (OPTIONAL) Draw or collage of what abundance feels like to you. Use colors, shapes, or images that represent how it would look and feel.

THE GIVING GAME

Self-love operates from a place of abundance and wholeness. When we practice self-love, we recognize that we already have everything we need inside ourselves. There's no need to look for validation or fulfillment externally because we've learned to see it in ourselves. From the perspective of the soul, our cup is already full, so to speak. Feeling gratitude for this fullness creates an inner peace that empowers us to perpetuate abundance and give freely to others.

Self-love isn't about indulging in endless spa treatments or girls' trips (although, seriously, treat yourself when you can). It's about nurturing the connection between the heart, mind, body, and soul. Unlike selfishness, which isolates, self-love connects. When your cup is full, you can share your talents, compassion, and love with others without feeling depleted or resentful. You give from a place of overflow, not lack.

Have you ever attended a speaking event where you felt drained after the speaker was done? That speaker likely came from a place of fear, needing your validation or acceptance. On the flip side, if you walked away feeling uplifted, the speaker likely spoke from a place of love, authenticity, and connection. Self-love allows you to create that same sense of abundance in your life.

"The first half of life is devoted to forming a healthy Ego; the second half is going inward and letting go of it."

- CARL JUNG

The Empathy & Self-Love Spectrum

Step 1: Below each scenario, mark the line where you fall on the empathy/self-love spectrum.

When your colleague asks you to stay late at work, but you've planned an evening at home. Think about this situations and mark where you usually fall on the spectrum:

Empathy for Others <--> **Self-Love**

Your partner is going through a tough time emotionally and wants your support, but you're dealing with your emotional struggles and need time to process them.

Empathy for Others <--> **Self-Love**

When a group of friends invites you to a social event, but you've been feeling overwhelmed and need some alone time to recharge.

Empathy for Others <--> **Self-Love**

When your child wants to spend extra time with you, and you need a break from parenting to focus on your own self-care.

Empathy for Others <--> **Self-Love**

Your community organization asks you to volunteer for an upcoming event, but you've already committed to personal growth activities.

Empathy for Others <--> **Self-Love**

Step 2: Next, use the following questions to reflect on the scenarios.

Based on where you fall on the scales, do you see yourself prioritizing others desires over yours or are you comfortable saying 'no' in any situation? Elaborate in the space below.

If you have trouble saying 'no,' think of a time when you gave too much and felt drained. What can you do differently?

List three ways you can give to others that feel joyful, easy, and fulfilling for you.

15-Minute Check-In

On days when giving of yourself feels heavy, use this quick check-in to reconnect with yourself and rebalance your energy.

To relax the mind, focus on the following breathing sequence. Repeat it three times, then check in with yourself by asking questions like, *"How am I feeling now?" "What do I need?"* Then, just notice and act on what comes to mind for you.

The breathing sequence is called Box Breathing. Repeat the four-step sequence three times.

The sequence goes as follows:

    1. Breathe slowly and deeply for three seconds.

    2. Relax, holding your breath for three seconds.

    3. Exhale your breath slowly and evenly for three seconds.

    4. Relax the body for three seconds before inhaling again.

GENUINE CONNECTION

We all have a dark side and weaknesses because we are all part of the human race. Carl Jung famously said, "Knowing your own darkness is the best method for dealing with the darkness of other people." Self-love invites you to explore your shadows—the parts of yourself you've been afraid to face or perhaps even ashamed of. Instead of judging yourself for these less-than-desirable traits, embrace them with kindness and compassion. Seeing your so-called flaws as part of your humanity rather than evidence of your unworthiness is a subtle perception shift with big payoffs.

As you become more accepting of your humanness, you naturally extend that same compassion to others. You stop seeing people as competitors or threats and start viewing them as fellow human beings, each navigating their struggles. This shift creates a profound connection with the people around you. Instead of putting up walls of judgment, you open doors of empathy. You understand that everyone is a work in progress, including you. And that's the beauty of self-love: it softens the way you relate to yourself and others.

In essence, self-love helps you meet people where they are (including yourself)—strengths, weaknesses, and everything in between. It creates a pathway for you to connect with that little girl inside in a truly meaningful way.

Another important aspect of self-love is its role in setting healthy boundaries. When you love and respect yourself, you can better protect your energy and mental health. This doesn't mean shutting people out. It means understanding your limits and core values and then ensuring you're not overextending yourself. Healthy boundaries and knowing what resonates with you are essential for maintaining deep, meaningful connections. By learning to take care of yourself, you avoid burnout and resentment, ensuring that giving to others is from a place of generosity rather than obligation.

Vulnerability as Strength

Step 1: Research shows that vulnerability fosters deep, meaningful connections. Self-love makes vulnerability safer because we are not seeking external validation.

Think about a relationship where you are afraid to be vulnerable and answer the following questions:

What fears keep me from revealing my true potential?

How can loving myself make it easier to share my true feelings?

Step 2: Next, take a small step toward vulnerability. This week, choose one person to practice a small act of vulnerability with. This step could be sharing a personal struggle or an unspoken need. Afterward, reflect and answer the following:

Did sharing deepen the relationship?

How did you feel after letting down your guard?

Step 3: Name one relationship where you feel like you can't be fully yourself. What's one way you can show up more authentically in that relationship?

Step 4: How do you think vulnerability changes the way you connect with others?

Adult Self Care Time

To fully show up in your life and for the people around you, it's important to carve out some 'me time.' Block out some time in your calendar, then pick out a cozy spot to read and work through the activities in this book. Think of this designated time and place as your personal power zone—like slipping into your favorite pair of jeans that makes you feel unstoppable.

Take time daily to recharge and center yourself. Sometimes, my power hour was at the beginning of the day, sometimes at the end of the day, and sometimes twice a day. My power hour has changed over the years based on my needs and so will yours.

HERE ARE SOME EXAMPLES FROM MY PLAYBOOK:

Example 1: 30 minutes of reading, 5 minutes of affirmations, 10 minutes of quiet breathing meditation, 15 minutes of journaling.

Example 2: 30 minutes of Yoga, 5 minutes of affirmations, 25 minutes of meditation or journaling.

Example 3: 1 full hour of quiet meditation while listening to relaxing music or nature sounds with headphones.

Tips for a successful Power Hour:

- Maintain a consistent schedule to get the benefits of a routine.
- Set boundaries with family members to ensure you have an uninterrupted hour.
- Personalize it.

Adapt the activities to fit your preferences and lifestyle. The key is to choose activities that resonate with you and provide a sense of fulfillment.

- Mindfulness or Meditation
- Physical Activity
- Intentional Planning
- Self-Care, Reflection, and Gratitude
- Journaling, Reading or Learning

Craft Your Self-Love Manifesto

Writing a manifesto will help you clarify what matters to you, empower you to make intentional choices, and keep you focused on your purpose. By articulating your principles, a personal manifesto acts as a reminder to stay true to your authentic self and live with greater confidence and direction. Refer back to it when life gets chaotic and challenging.

Include the following in your manifesto:

- Three core beliefs about yourself that support your self-love.
- Three beliefs you want to release.

Daily Intention Pause

A daily practice to increase awareness of intention is a simple mindful practice called "Intention Pause." It is a two-part practice designed to be integrated into the morning and evening. In the morning, set an intention to notice motivations throughout the day, focusing on love vs. fear. In the evening, briefly reflect on the moments when your ego or soul guided you.

This simple but consistent practice can deepen self-love by helping you cultivate mindfulness around your motivations. By setting intentions and reflecting on them regularly, you'll begin to naturally recognize what motivates you throughout the day, creating more opportunities to grow.

Step 1: Morning Intention Setting (Takes about 5 minutes)

Find a quiet moment: Sit comfortably, close your eyes, and take a few deep breaths.

Set an Intention: Set a simple, clear intention to identify your motivations today. For example you could say silently: *"Today, I intend to notice whether my actions are led by love or fear, abundance or scarcity."*

Choose a Loving Anchor Question: Select a question that reminds you of your intention throughout the day. Some examples: *"Am I acting from love?"*, *"Am I being guided by abundance or scarcity?"*, *"What would love choose?"*

Visualize Acting with Love: Spend a moment visualizing yourself throughout the day, making choices from love, compassion, and abundance toward yourself. This visualization can set a powerful mental tone for your day.

Reminder Tip: Set a reminder on your phone or place a sticky note with your anchor question somewhere visible to prompt you to periodically check in on your intentions.

Step 2: Evening Reflection (About 5-10 Minutes)

Take a few minutes to reflect on your motivation. Be gentle with yourself and over the coming weeks, increase awareness without judgment. You might find it helpful to keep a journal nearby for this reflection.

Recall the Day's Actions: Briefly scan the day, noting key actions or interactions.

Identify Motivations: For each action, ask yourself: *"Was this motivated by ego (fear, scarcity, need for control) or by soul (love, generosity, wholeness)?"*

If you find ego motivations, consider whether a specific fear, insecurity, or worry is driving you. Be curious, not critical.

Celebrate Moments of Love and Soul-Led Action: Take note of actions from a place of love and abundance. Recognize and affirm them, even if they seem small, as these choices express self-love.

Set a Gentle Goal for Tomorrow: End your reflection by setting a goal or affirmation for the next day, such as *"Tomorrow, I'll look for more moments to choose love"* or *"I am capable of making choices that nourish myself.*

BOTTOM LINE

Healthy self-love is like lighting candles on a grand chandelier—when you share your flame with others, your light doesn't diminish; it expands. By loving yourself first, you ignite an overflow of love, compassion, and authenticity that touches everyone around you. Self-love isn't selfish; it fuels connection, resilience, and joy. It creates wholeness, confidence, and peace.

When grounded in the soul, self-love transforms the way we experience life. Instead of operating from a place of scarcity or fear, we embrace an abundance mindset and lifestyle that reminds us there's more than enough love, success, and happiness to go around. This shift allows us to fill our cups and give freely to others without feeling depleted. Self-love, when nurtured, turns us into beacons of light—strong enough to weather life's storms yet gentle enough to spark warmth in others.

"From the perspective of the Ego, uncertainty breeds fear.
From the perspective of the Soul, it breeds nothing but possibility."

- Peter Crone

CHAPTER TWO

Peeling Back the Ego

02

To truly flourish after fifty, it's essential to understand the forces that shape our lives. That's where the ego and the soul come into play. Midlife is a good time for integrating our humanness with our being-ness. In other words, it's time to dial back the ego and put the soul in the driver's seat.

Carl Jung, one of the great minds of psychology, developed the Theory of Individuation, which helps us unravel some of the mysteries of the mind. It sounds science-y, I know, but stay with me. The ego isn't just a fancy concept—it's the part of us that starts forming early in life, around the age of two, when we first begin to realize we are separate humans. This realization is the birth of the ego, and from that point on, it tries to protect us by helping us navigate the world. The ego is our survival mechanism, it is rooted in fear, safety, and separation. It's the *"human"* part of the *Human Being*.

The *"being"* part of the *Human Being* is formed before birth. It is our soul—our true essence, and it is rooted in love. Love is more than an emotion; it is a force. It connects us to the divine, to one another, and to all of creation. Living from the soul's perspective, we operate from higher emotions and vibrations like love, joy, and abundance. These emotions feel natural because they align with our authentic state of being. They nurture genuine connections with ourselves and others.

In a nutshell, a Human Being is more than a physical body. Remember the Wayne Dyer quote in the introduction about spiritual beings having a human experience? This body is the union between ego and soul. When they are integrated in a healthy way, we rise above challenges and flourish. To understand these two very different parts of yourself, let's explore the characteristics of both.

Reflect on Your Persona

Start by thinking about the persona you've built over the years—the roles, masks, and expectations you've collected like souvenirs. This is the version of you that the world sees, and it's been shaped by all sorts of external pressures. Now, take a deep breath, reflect on the following questions, and write down your answers.

What roles do you play in your life? (e.g., mother, professional, caretaker)

How do you believe others see you?

What do your friends say about you (in terms of your qualities, characteristics, etc.)?

What do you believe is expected of you in these roles?

Do you feel genuine in these roles or feel like you're playing a part?

THE TWO SIDES OF HUMAN BEINGS

One of the most important realizations in the journey of self-love and transformation is understanding the parts of the Self and how they shape our lives—the ego and the soul. These two components express vastly different worldviews, perspectives, and emotional experiences. Understanding how they influence us and learning to harmonize and integrate them are the keys to living a more fulfilled, authentic life, especially in midlife. Why? Because in midlife, we've lived long enough in our human conditioning that the ego has built up quit a crust of layers around our souls.

Think of the ego as similar to fat in the body. A small percentage of fat is healthy and necessary for a healthy body. If we avoid movement and eat unhealthy foods on a regular basis, over time, the fat builds up in our bodies, causing diseases. Likewise, continuing to operate with belief systems and coping mechanisms formed by the ego in childhood establishes decisions based in reaction instead of creation.

These ego-driven decisions generate a mindset based on lack and negativity rather than abundance and positivity. They are rooted in the fear of a helpless child, not a mature adult who can create their life. For example, if as a child, you formed the belief, *"I need to be seen and not heard to make mom and dad happy,"* as an adult, you might decide not to express your views in meetings or communicate your boundaries in relationships. Instead, you quietly internalize and/or repress your ideas, feelings, wants, and needs.

To experience this world, we need both the ego and the soul, but each has a different role. What does it mean to be an integrated *Human Being*? The ego and the soul have very different origins, jobs, and characteristics. Learning the attributes of each will help you identify which one is leading, and more importantly, how to shift from the ego's overactive perspective to the soul's love-based truth.

Characteristics	Human = Ego	Being = Soul
World View	Rooted in Fear & Scarcity Limited Potential	Rooted in Love & Abundance Limitless Potential
Designed for	Separation	Connection
Typical Emotional State	Low Vibration Emotions Familiar Uncomfortable	High Vibration Emotions Resonate
Origin	Formed After Birth Human Creation	Formed Before Birth Divine Authenticity
Effect on the body	Sympathetic Nervous System (Fight, Flight, or Freeze Response)	Balance of Sympathetic Nervous System & Parasympathetic Nervous System

CHARACTERISTICS OF THE EGO

As stated earlier, the ego is a survival mechanism that forms in early childhood, usually around the age of two, when we begin to see ourselves as separate from others. While the ego's role is to protect and help us survive, it often operates from a place of fear and scarcity. When it believes we are separate, we must compete for resources and defend ourselves against loss or harm. Here's how the Ego shapes our world:

Worldview Rooted in Fear: The ego's perspective is deeply influenced by fear—fear of rejection, fear of failure, fear of not being enough, and fear of losing control, among others. These fears often stem from early experiences that shaped our sense of self and safety in the world. The ego convinces us that we must work endlessly, compete with others, and constantly prove our worth to secure physical survival. It's scarcity-driven mindset keeps us focused on what we lack and what we must protect rather than what we already have or who we truly are.

Designed for Separation: The ego develops behaviors and beliefs aimed at helping us navigate the world and stay safe by predicting potential threats and protecting us from harm. It engages our Sympathetic Nervous System—the fight, flight, or freeze response—often keeping us in a heightened state of stress. One of the ego's primary tools is judgment. By labeling people, situations, and even ourselves as "good" or "bad," "right" or "wrong," the ego attempts to create a sense of control and certainty in an unpredictable world. However, this constant judging often fosters feelings of disconnection, loneliness, and inadequacy, as it reinforces the idea that we are separate and must protect ourselves from others or prove our worth.

Low-Vibration Emotions: The ego lives in a world of low-vibration emotions—anger, insecurity, jealousy, and shame (just to name a few). These emotions are uncomfortable because they are out of alignment with our authenticity. Yet, the ego clings to them because they are familiar and it's trying to keep us safe. The ironic thing is, left unchecked, we are caught in a vicious cycle of these low-vibrational emotions and energies creating more separation. The ego requires external validation or stimuli to temporarily experience high-vibration emotions.

Formed After Birth: The ego is a construct that forms after birth as we interact with the world, pick up beliefs from others, and learn to navigate society. It is informed and shaped by our environment, not by our source.

Limited Perspective: The ego has a narrow, limited view of reality. Because it is designed to protect us, it views the world from the perspective of lack instead of abundance. The ego struggles to see beyond itself and can trap the mind in a loop.

While the ego is often associated with fear and limitation, it also has positive attributes that play an important role in our growth and development. A healthy dose of ego serves a purpose. Just like fat cells store energy and protect vital organs, the ego helps us establish a sense of identity, navigate social interactions, and stay motivated to achieve goals. For example, the ego might push us to prepare for a presentation, ensuring we perform well and make a positive impression. When kept in check (like fat in a healthy body), the ego can be useful for building confidence and resilience. The key is to recognize its role without letting it dominate, allowing us to make decisions from a place of confidence and authenticity rather than fear.

Exploring the Inner Critic

Take time to reflect on the thoughts that arise when you look at yourself in the mirror. Do these thoughts feel like judgments? Write them down, but don't try to replace or push them away. Just allow them to exist on the page without reacting.

The purpose of this exercise is to explore your inner dialogue without judgment. Honesty and awareness are the keys to releasing these thoughts, not through force but through understanding and compassion for yourself.

Ask yourself:

Where do these beliefs come from?

How do these judgments shape the way I see myself?

Can I hold space for these thoughts without needing to change them?'

CHARACTERISTICS OF THE SOUL

While the ego operates from a foundation of fear, comparison, and separation, the soul stands firmly rooted in love, unity, and universal truth. It is the timeless part of us that existed before we took our first breath and will endure beyond our last. The soul is the essence of who we truly are, unencumbered by the human masks we wear or the roles we play. It connects us to something far greater than ourselves.

This connection transcends humanness, offering a source of unconditional love, guidance, and wisdom. The soul is the inner compass pointing us toward a path of growth and fulfillment, the "true north" that aligns with our deepest values and purpose. While the ego thrives on external validation, the soul finds fulfillment in simply *being human*. Other than expressing unconditional love, the soul has no agenda.

By tapping into the still small but powerful voice of the soul, we reconnect with our authenticity, our inherent worth, and the interconnectedness of all things. Whether we experience it in moments of stillness, awe, or love, the soul invites us to live from a place of wholeness and to trust in the boundless potential already inside us.

HERE'S HOW THE SOUL INFLUENCES US:

Worldview Rooted in Love: The soul offers unlimited perspectives. It understands that we are infinite beings, capable of boundless love, creativity, and expansion. The soul sees the bigger picture and knows everything unfolds for our highest good. This broader perspective helps us trust the journey and diminishes the power of fear.

Designed for Connection: Unlike the ego, which thrives on separation and competition, the soul is wired for unity. It recognizes the harmony in all things and operates from compassion, kindness, and peace. The soul encourages us to see beyond differences and embrace the interconnectedness of life, allowing us to form deeper relationships.

High-Vibration Emotions: The soul resonates naturally with high-vibration emotions like joy, peace, and love because they feel like home. These states of being flow instinctively and resonate with us because they reflect our true nature. Unlike the ego, which craves external validation to feel good, the soul's well-being is intrinsic and self-sustaining.

Timeless and Eternal: The soul is not a product of the world—it existed before birth and will continue to exist. It is timeless and unchanging, rooted in divine authenticity. The soul is the purest expression of Self, untainted by the fears and limitations of the ego.

Limitless Perspective: The soul offers unlimited perspectives. It understands that we are infinite beings, capable of boundless love and creativity. The soul sees the bigger picture and knows everything unfolds for our highest good. This broader perspective helps us trust the journey and tap into our potential.

Living from the soul's perspective transforms how we experience life, shifting us from struggling through life to thriving. This alignment allows us to flow naturally with life's rhythm rather than resisting it. In the flow state—marked by timelessness, focus, and effortless engagement—we access the origin of creativity and inner peace that makes challenges feel manageable and achievements deeply fulfilling. Life feels lighter because we're no longer weighed down by unnecessary fears or an incessant need for external validation. Instead, we embrace our inherent worth and the freedom to live authentically.

When surrendering to the soul, we develop a profound resilience that keeps us from getting stuck in negativity when life throws us a curveball. The soul sees beyond temporary setbacks, offering a broader perspective that reminds us everything unfolds for our highest good. This ability to reframe difficulties as opportunities for growth allows us to bounce back more quickly and with greater clarity.

This connection to the soul also brings physical and emotional balance. Living in alignment helps regulate the nervous system, achieving harmony between the sympathetic (fight, flight, or freeze) and the parasympathetic (rest, digest, and create) systems. This balance reduces stress, lowers cortisol levels, and enhances overall well-being, creating a calm yet energized state of being. This physiological stability equips us to navigate life's ups and downs with clarity and grace, stimulating a sense of inner strength, confidence, and resilience.

Ultimately, living from the soul increases our resilience and deepens our connection with others and our capacity for joy. By viewing life through the lens of love and abundance, we find purpose and meaning even in the mundane. We trust the journey, embrace our creativity, and approach life as an ever-evolving masterpiece. Whether we're soaring through life's highs or navigating its inevitable lows, the soul ensures we remain grounded in love, open to possibility, and ready to grow.

Embodying the "I Am Free" Mindset

For this exercise you will need a calm quiet place to do some visualization and deep reflective work.

Instead of creating affirmations that push you toward self-improvement, practice simply sitting with the idea that you are free from the need to be anything other than what you are right now (a creative being in a body).

Place your hand over your heart, take a few deep breaths, and allow yourself to feel that freedom. Spend some time feeling gratitude for the different aspects of yourself. If you come to a part of yourself you find difficult to feel gratitude for, just make a note without judgment. Spend as much time as you need on this step. Make some notes after each question.

As you reflect, ask yourself questions like:

How does it feel to let go of judgment, even for just a moment?

What emotions or sensations arise when I accept myself exactly as I am?

Can I allow this moment of being enough to simply exist without needing to change it?

Where did I feel resistance to gratitude or freedom? Why?

What emotions, sensations, or memories came up during this exercise?

How does this experience differ from the way you usually think about yourself?

Soul Alignment Visualization

This exercise bridges the gap between understanding the soul conceptually and experiencing it emotionally. It will require you to find a comfortable and quiet place without distractions.

Close your eyes and visualize yourself living entirely from your soul. Imagine a day where every decision and interaction comes from unconditional love, joy, and abundance. Spend as much time as you need with the visualization. Write down what this looks and feels like.

Ho'oponopono Meditation

Ho'oponopono is a simple Hawaiian healing practice. It's a beautiful way to help release any lingering judgment and make space for your precious soul. Here we go:

- If you like, put on some relaxing background music or nature sounds.
- Find a comfortable position. Lying down or sitting in a quiet place where you won't be disturbed.
- Either close your eyes or find one focal point.
- Relax your mind and body with a few deep breaths and focus on the present.

Repeat the following aloud or in your mind:

"I love you. I'm sorry. Please forgive me. Thank you."

During this phase of the meditation different memories, emotions, or physical sensations will pop up. Let them, but do not attach to them or try to work through them. Inject the four sentences into what came up for you and keep repeating them until you feel a release. If you don't feel a release, try again in a future session.

Here's an example of how the meditation typically goes: Let's say a memory of an argument pops up while you repeat the four sentences. The memory might be about getting bullied. It was a time when you didn't stand up for yourself. Say the four sentences while recalling the memory. Keep repeating them until you feel a release physically, mentally, or emotionally. When you are ready, repeat the same process with the memories of people who hurt you.

Self-Reflection in the Mirror

In this exercise, you'll use the mirror as a tool to look beyond your physical reflection and uncover the thoughts, emotions, and judgments that shape how you see yourself. This practice aligns with the deeper work of peeling back the ego. By observing yourself without criticism or attachment, you'll begin to witness not just who you are on the outside but the parts of yourself you may have buried or overlooked.

Step 1: Begin by setting a timer for 5-15 minutes. Sit comfortably in front of a mirror and look into your own eyes. Take a few deep breaths to calm your mind and center yourself. As you look at yourself, try to simply observe without judgment. Notice what thoughts or emotions arise when you see yourself in the mirror. Don't label these thoughts as good or bad—just allow them to come in and out of your awareness.

Step 2: When the timer goes off, write down or draw your thoughts, feelings, and any judgments that came up during the exercise. Don't filter or analyze them; just let them flow onto the page. It doesn't matter if they make sense; just write whatever comes to mind uninterrupted for at least five minutes. The goal here is not to correct or change anything but to become aware of your current state.

Step 3: After journaling for five minutes, consider the following reflection questions:
- Who am I beyond my roles and responsibilities?
- What emotions or sensations arise when I look at myself in the mirror?
- What thoughts pop up when I look in the mirror?
- Can I observe without needing to change or fix anything?
- How does it feel to live life with the feeling of being unworthy?
- What might be possible if I'm not living in a place of unworthiness?

Step 4: Next, reflect on the mirror exercise and answer the following:

What words or phrases come to mind when you look at yourself in the mirror?

Do these thoughts align more with "becoming" (future-focused, striving), "being" (present, accepting), or "been" (past thoughts)?

Thought or Emotion	Being	Becoming	Been

How does this inner dialogue make you feel? It's important to note your inner dialogue often. When we identify a false belief from childhood, we can expose and take away its power. A sadness for the loss of life or not living up to our potential is normal. Or, you may experience lightness instead of sadness. Whatever comes up, let yourself feel the feelings without judgment.

Practice "Being" Instead of "Fixing"

For the next week, commit to observing yourself without trying to change or fix anything. Each morning, stand in front of the mirror, look into your eyes, and remind yourself that you are already the best version of yourself. Notice how this shift feels as you go about your day.

Throughout the day, remind yourself that you are enough, especially when struggling or self-criticizing. If you struggle, check in with yourself and ask questions like: *"What do I want or need this moment to be at my best?"* You might need more rest or exercise. Your body might be craving certain food, or your mind might need peace and quiet. Try stepping outside for a walk to get away from a chatty colleague at work.

At the end of each day, reflect on your experience:

Did you practice self-acceptance?

How did letting go of judgment affect your day?

Did you notice any changes in your self-talk or emotions?

What challenges did you face in simply being without trying to fix or improve yourself?

Live From the Soul

At the end of the week, revisit the reflection question in the workbook and reflect on the experience of letting go of judgment and self-acceptance. Consider how inner freedom has shifted your perception of yourself.

What have you learned about the difference between judgment and acceptance?

How has the perception of yourself changed since beginning this activity?

What have you learned about the difference between "becoming" and "being"?

BOTTOM LINE

Things shift once you realize you're more than just a body with an ego. You're a soul in a body with limitless potential. Living from your higher self means ditching the outdated programs created by the ego that no longer serve you. Stop trying to fit into someone else's mold. Your soul knows the way, like a GPS with all the right directions. The route will look different for everyone, but we all have the same tools inside us.

So, instead of looking at life through the ego's distorted perspective, why not see it through the eyes of your soul? The difference is transformative. You stop worrying about what people think, and you start getting curious about what really lights you up. What do you love or not? What feels off? And, most importantly, why?

In other words, observe without judgment. Yes, I know, that's like asking you to walk out the door without mascara—but trust me, it's worth the effort. Combining self-awareness with self-compassion doesn't mean adopting a new label; it means shedding the labels to reveal the authentic you underneath. Every time you release judgment and peel back one more layer of ego, you have a better view of your true self. You'll see that you don't need to patch or perfect a thing; underneath all those ego-built defenses, you're already whole—no extra accessories required. Think of it like decluttering: each layer you let go of frees up a little more space for joy, self-compassion, and inner peace.

When we put the ego in the back seat (calmly assuring it that, no, there's no need to check every mirror or count the exits), we let the soul take the wheel. Life shifts from a never-ending survival marathon to something lighter, fun, and a lot more interesting! It becomes a celebration.

"Ego says, 'Once everything falls into place, I'll feel peace.' Spirit says, 'Find your peace, and then everything will fall into place.'"

- MARIANNE WILLIAMSON

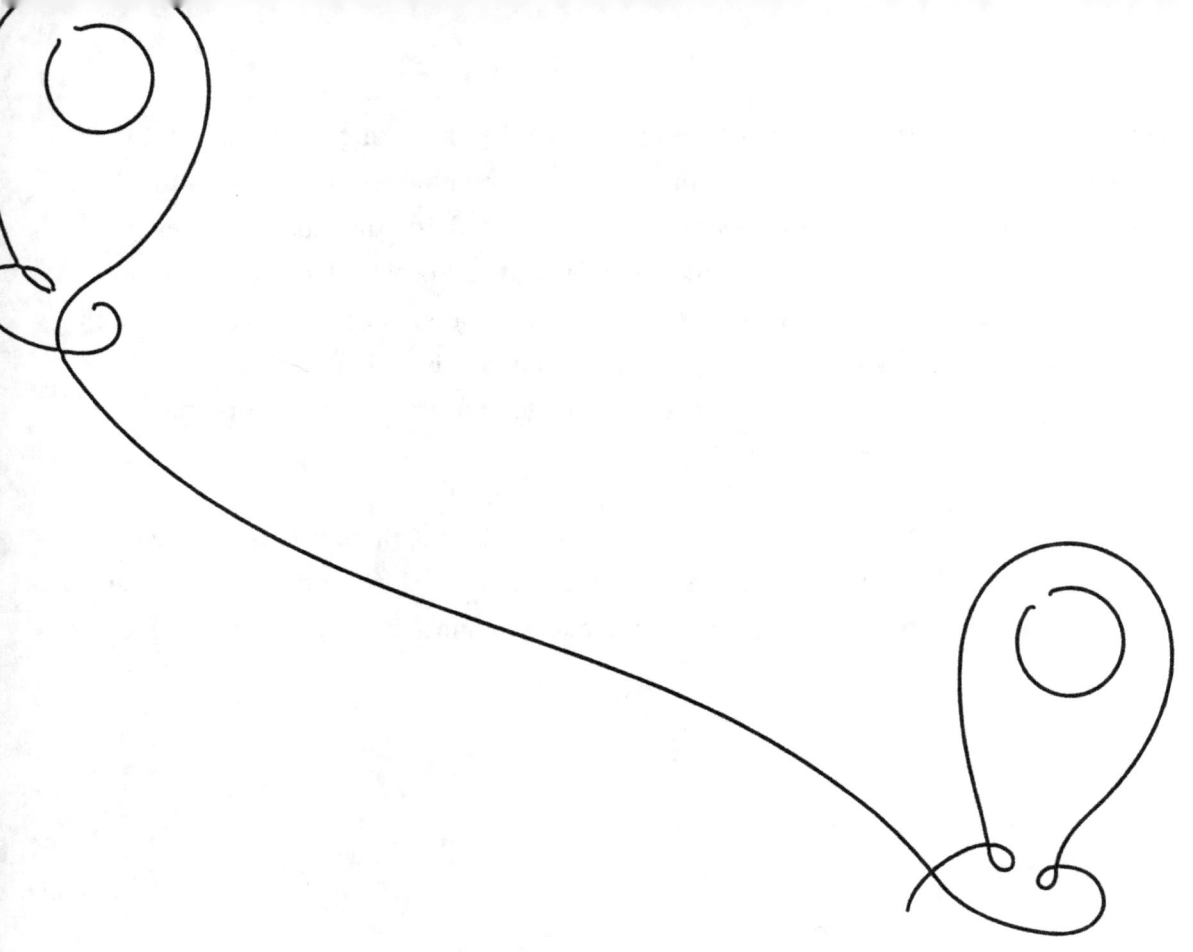

"Your core values are the deeply held beliefs that authentically describe your soul."

- John C. Maxwell

03

CHAPTER THREE

Inner GPS

It's funny how many deep self-reflective moments pop up during midlife. Have you ever experienced looking in the mirror and thinking, *"Who is that?' or "Where did **she** go?"* It happened to me. One morning, during my typical hygiene routine, I looked in the mirror and saw more laugh lines and crow's feet than I remember earning. The dull eyes, thinning hair, and permanent worry lines across my forehead made me look like my grandmother. I remember thinking, *"Yikes! When did this happen?"* I don't remember the exact moment the woman I used to see slipped away, but I'm pretty sure it was sometime after I started caring more about my cholesterol level than about climbing trees.

Love has a way of bringing us back to ourselves when we get lost. For me, life piled on the problems until I was in survival mode, living with childhood wounds and pulling from immature coping mechanisms. Those dated strategies worked beautifully when I was little, but as an adult, they sent me into panic attacks, rumination, low self-esteem, and isolation. My ego was in overdrive, hijacking my inner GPS and setting it to the wrong destination. I was backtracking instead of growing, operating in pure fear instead of in alignment with my soul. My life purpose was left in the dust, not even visible in the rearview mirror.

Evaluate Your Current Situation

The following exercise will help give you a picture of what is going on in your life at this time. Values can fluctuate throughout life as we accomplish goals, learn, and change. Knowing what life looks like for you now helps.

Step 1: Record a brief description of what is going on in your life right now in the following areas:

Business:

Family:

Spiritual:

Financial:

Physical Health:

Social/Friendships:

Mental Health:

Step 2: Jot down five things you currently find difficult or stressful. These could be external circumstances, internal struggles, or habits that make your life harder.

Step 3: List five things or people that provide you with stability or positive reinforcement. Think of the people who encourage you, activities that bring you peace, or resources you can lean on for guidance or support.

Step 4: It's time to tally up your answers. In the first column below, list the responses by topic. Record the number of times a topic is mentioned in the middle column. In the last column, give each topic a number value based on the number of times you listed it in the questions— 1 equals the most mentioned topic.

Topic	Number of Times Mentioned	Order of Value to You

ANCHORED IN PURPOSE

Part of living life at the soul level is identifying core values. You may already be aligned with religion, society, or family-supported values. However, all the external influences can leave you out of alignment with your true inner compass. Motivation, creativity, and productivity naturally follow when you act in harmony with your core values. They are part of our built-in Genuine Path to Self or inner GPS. They steer us away from the ego's need for shallow gratification and toward our soul's purpose.

The morning I found myself looking at someone else in the mirror, it was more than just my physical appearance that changed. I couldn't remember who I was apart from my roles of wife and mother. I only brought a part of myself to these roles. The quest to find the missing core of my identity required gagging the backseat driver (ego), which led me to rediscover my core values.

Remember the movie where Julia Roberts played a bride who never made it down the aisle? She always changed what she liked and didn't like to match her romantic partner. She didn't even know how she preferred her breakfast eggs. So, next time you order eggs, think of it as a values test!

"We are never more fully alive, more completely ourselves, or more deeply engrossed in anything than when we are playing."

- CHARLES SCHAEFER

Core Values Assessment

Living authentically means tossing out the cookie cutter and getting comfy with your wild side. Know yourself, moles and all, and accept that the person in the mirror was put here with purpose. Packed within each of us is a treasure chest of gifts and talents—not intended to sit collecting dust in the attic but to be unpacked and put to work.

Discovering your life purpose starts with a treasure hunt where X marks the spot on your values. Not the values the world subscribes to, but the ones that make your heart sing. Identifying and getting acquainted with your core values is essential. Embrace who you are, not who everyone else expects you to be. Authenticity is not a one-size-fits-all but is tailor-made. Own it!

Step 1: To embark on the adventure for life's purpose, using our GPS (Genuine Path to Self) navigation, we begin by mapping out core values. So, grab your favorite pen and jot down a 2-6 word answer to the following questions. This isn't a term paper. Your answers need to be short and to the point.

Look around your work or home space. List the top three things most prominently displayed. These items can have sentimental, monetary, or inspirational values.

Name the top three ways you like to spend your time.

Name the top three things that energize you the most. (What gets you up in the morning?)

What are the top three ways you spend your money? Not bills and mortgage but hobbies, travel, home improvements (if you enjoy that), and groceries might count if you enjoy cooking and throwing dinner parties.

When we value something, it is easier to stay organized because we enjoy doing it. Name the top three areas in which you are best organized.

In what area are you the most disciplined and focused? Or, where are you the most reliable?

Excluding negative self-talk, what do you think about the most? What shows up in your life as a result of loving thoughts? What do you manifest?

Name the top three things you visualize the most. What do you imagine the most?

What do you internally dialogue with yourself about the most? Excluding ruminating on past dramas or negative self-talk?

In social settings, what do you talk about the most? Or What can you talk about for hours with no preparation?

What do you find the most inspiring? What moves you?

Think about long-term goals. Ones you have achieved and even ones you have not achieved yet. What are consistently the top three?

What do you enjoy learning about the most? What podcasts do you listen to? What topics do you read about?

Step 2: Use the word bank below or make up your own to help identify the core values that resonate most with your soul. Refer back to the thirteen questions you answered in the last exercise for clues to what might be important to you. Then, circle your top 5–7 core values.

Curiosity · Wisdom · Open-mindedness · Learning · Self-Development · Creativity
Innovation · Adventure · Exploration · Connection & Relationships · Love
Compassion · Empathy · Family · Friendship · Community · Loyalty · Belonging
Trust · Intimacy · Character · Honesty · Integrity · Authenticity · Accountability
Responsibility · Courage · Honor · Humility · Justice · Fairness
Wellness & Balance · Health & Vitality · Balance · Peace · Rest · Simplicity · Freedom
Self-Care · Patience · Mindfulness · Purpose & Impact · Purpose, Meaning · Service
Contribution · Leadership · Influence · Legacy · Generosity · Volunteerism
Mentorship · Achievement & Drive · Ambition, Success · Determination · Motivation
Excellence · Mastery · Perseverance · Spontaneity · Choice · Uniqueness
Security & Stability · Safety · Comfort · Consistency · Predictability · Order
Structure · Organization · Tradition

Step 3: Record below your top core values:

Next, reflect on how your current life aligns with these values. Are you living in alignment with what matters most? If not, what small changes could you make to honor these values more fully?

LIVING AUTHENTICALLY THROUGH YOUR VALUES

When you find yourself in front of the mirror, feeling frustrated for not meeting your expectations, pause and ask, *"What can I learn from this frustration? What is it revealing to me?"* The lessons learned during these moments often propel you toward living out your core values more fully. Every experience, whether it feels like a success or a setback, serves as a stepping stone toward greater alignment with your highest Self.

Not only do core values play a role in your daily life, they are great for setting long term goals that reflect your authenticity. The beauty of setting goals based on core values is that the journey itself becomes enjoyable, even if you hit a few bumps along the way. The goal is no longer about reaching a destination to prove yourself; it's about expanding and expressing your unique gifts and talents. After all, nobody can do it like you? Check out the sampling of people I know and how they live out their core values.

Morals and core values are two different things. Morals like honesty and compassion can be part of the broader spectrum of values that drive you. Core values are deeply held principles of what is instinctually important to you and how you prioritize it. Here are a few examples of what I mean...

My husband, Steve, deeply respects nature, particularly marine life. He often feels the need to be out on the ocean, deep-sea fishing. The thrill of the catch is only part of what he enjoys— connecting with the sea and marine life gives him a sense of peace and clarity. This core value also drives him to speak up about environmental issues concerning ocean life and help with conservation efforts. Steve's commitment to the ocean is more than a hobby; it's how he feels at home.

I'm passionate about education and diversity. Even in the face of social backlash, the fact that I didn't have a formal teaching degree didn't hold back my drive to homeschool my children. My core values also shine through as I learn about and connect with people from different backgrounds and countries when I travel. Sharing what I learn with others is at my core. Speaking and writing are more than hobbies—they're ways I live out who I'm created to be.

Then there's my mother. She has a deep-seated passion for creativity and self-expression. Her art room looks like an exploded craft store—it's a treasure trove of art supplies and projects.

For Mom, making things with her hands isn't just a pastime; it's how she shares beauty with the world. Her core values are creativity and self-expression, and she's happiest when she's knee-deep in a new project, losing track of time.

My mother-in-law, Marquita, values community and connection. She organizes gatherings, checks in on old friends, and volunteers at the local not-for-profit secondhand book store. Helping others and fostering a sense of belonging are her core values. She finds joy and fulfillment in these activities, and it's clear that she's living her values every day.

And then there's my sister, Leighsa, who values health and wellness above all. She's the one who convinced me to incorporate exercise into my day (which I used to hate but now I look forward to it). Leighsa is always reading up on the latest health trends, meal-prepping like a pro, and encouraging everyone around her to take better care of themselves. Her dedication to health and wellness is a core value that drives her daily decisions and activities.

Realignment Action Plan

Step 1: Choose one area of your life where you'd like to bring more alignment with your core values. Write down a specific action you can take to honor this value more fully in your daily life. Consider starting with small, manageable changes that can lead to a greater sense of fulfillment.

Example:

Core Value: Health and wellness

Area of Life: Daily routine

Specific Action: Incorporate a 20-minute morning walk into my routine three times a week.

Time Frame: Start next Monday

Now it's your turn:

Core Value:

Area of Life:

Specific Action:

Time Frame:

Core Value:

Area of Life:

Specific Action:

Time Frame:

Core Value:

Area of Life:

Specific Action:

Time Frame:

Core Value:

Area of Life:

Specific Action:

Time Frame:

Values-Based Goal Mapping

Connect core values to realistic, soul-aligned goals.

Write down your top core values. Brainstorm 2–3 soul-aligned goals that reflect each value and jot them down.

Soul-Aligned Goal #1

Soul-Aligned Goal#2

Soul- Aligned Goal#3

Reflection Prompt:

Which of these goals excites you the most?

How can you start working toward one goal this week?

BOTTOM LINE

Midlife is the perfect time to ask yourself: *How do I like my eggs?* Seriously. Just like Julia Roberts' character. Discovering your preferences—your real preferences—is key to uncovering your core values. It's not about what your partner, your boss, or society thinks you should want. It's about what makes you feel alive, aligned, and deeply fulfilled.

Start with those little things that bring you joy, and let them lead you to the bigger picture. Spend time figuring out what truly matters to you and let go of chasing ego-driven goals that leave you feeling emptier than a plate of cold scrambled eggs. Your core values are the soul lovingly saying, *"Hey, this is who you really are."*

So, whether you're a poached, fried, or over-easy kind of person, make sure your choices reflect you. Here's to ignoring the ego's nagging backseat directions and letting your soul lead you to your most fulfilling, sunny-side-up life!

"The greatest freedom is the freedom to choose
who you become in this moment."

- Unknown

04

CHAPTER FOUR

Free Your Mind

L et's talk about my friend Sarah. From the outside, her life looked like a Pinterest board of success—a stable career, a great husband, and two teenagers who mostly did their homework. But on the inside? It was a whole other story. Sarah felt stuck in a weird limbo of *"I **should** be happy"* mixed with *"Why do I feel so meh?"* Every day was a marathon—keeping the peace, juggling work, family, and whatever else life threw her way. She kept telling herself, *"Be grateful; I'm living the dream,"* but deep down, she couldn't shake the feeling she was living someone else's life.

Then, one evening, scrolling through social media (as one does when life feels too much but not enough), Sarah stumbled across a post about how childhood beliefs shape adulthood. One line practically leaped off the screen: *"The stories we carry from childhood become the prisons we live in as adults."* It was like a lightbulb turned on in her head.

For the first time, Sarah asked herself, *"Wait...what story have I been living in?"* She thought back to her childhood when love often felt like a performance review. Her parents were kind but distant; praise mainly showed up when she aced a test or behaved perfectly. Her mistakes were usually met with side-eye and disappointment. Sarah had learned early on: *To feel worthy, you've got to perform, achieve, and keep everything under control.*

And there it was—the invisible bars of her mental prison. The beliefs *"I'm only valuable if I'm productive"* and *"I must always improve"* have been running the show for decades. It explained her constant overworking, her fear of failure, and why relaxing felt foreign. Sarah realized she wasn't entirely living a full life; she was living a life shaped by an old, invisible script.

REACTIVITY

Most of us are walking around inside a mental prison of our own making. These cages were built way back when we were kids before we even knew what was happening. You didn't have to grow up in a toxic home with an alcoholic parent to develop childhood coping mechanisms that turned into adult limiting beliefs. Maybe you grew up with parents who yelled at each other, and your brain decided, *"The world isn't safe; I always have to be on guard."* Or maybe you faced criticism for being a rowdy kid and internalized the *"I'm not good enough"* mantra. These stories don't stay in the past—they hitch a ride into adulthood, quietly running the show from the subconscious.

Old coping mechanisms show up when you freeze on a simple decision, terrified of making the wrong choice. They show up when you say "yes" to things you don't want to do because rejection feels unbearable. They show up when you pick a safe path instead of chasing that thing that makes your heart sing.

Living reactively means your mind is set on cruise control, programmed by the fears and beliefs you picked up in childhood. Instead of steering intentionally, you're coasting down a road paved by old patterns, unable to change direction even when the path you're on leads somewhere you don't want to go.

And guess what? Fears never take you anywhere fun. Reactivity leaves you feeling exhausted, anxious, confused, and resentful. You behave as if you're a passenger instead of the driver of your own life. With every twist and turn, life feels like a constant battle—putting out fires, meeting expectations, and trying to avoid rejection or failure, all while the cruise control keeps you stuck in the same repetitive loop.

What if you don't have to live like that? What if you could step out of the cage entirely? Instead of reacting to life's challenges using patterns from the past, what if you could create with intention a life that feels free, joyful, and completely you?

For Sarah, just the recognition of her prison bars was freeing—but also a little terrifying. What do you even do with that kind of ' aha moment'? She felt a shift in her energy, like a space opened up inside of her. It reminded her of when she cleaned the refrigerator. Getting rid of the old dated food, wiping everything down, and only putting back what her family can eat was refreshing and satisfying. Sarah didn't have all the answers, but she decided she couldn't keep pretending everything was fine. So, she started small.

One day, a coworker asked her to take on another project. Sarah's autopilot would normally kick in: *"Say yes, stay helpful, don't let anyone down."* But this time, she paused. She thought about that old belief trying to hijack her decision: *"If you don't do it, you'll disappoint them. You'll seem weak."* Instead, she took a deep breath and said, *"I can't take that on right now, but I'd love to help brainstorm some ideas."*

And guess what? The world didn't end. No one was mad. She wasn't struck by lightning for setting a boundary. Instead, she felt something she hadn't felt in years—a little bit of freedom.

Encouraged, Sarah started exploring this new approach in other areas of her life. She began journaling each morning, asking herself: *"Who am I when I'm not trying to prove my worth?"* Turns out, under all that perfectionism was someone wildly creative and curious. She even picked up painting again—a hobby she'd ditched in her twenties because it felt impractical. Slowly but surely, she began to rebuild her life—not in a constant performance, but as an honest expression of her core values.

"The way you treat your own heart is the way you
will end up treating everyone else's."

- JOHN ELDRIGDE

Spotting Your Mental Prison

Let's begin by identifying your stories. These stories are what you tell yourself, your conditioned beliefs. To truly step into the creative path, you must first examine what's holding you back and find its root.

Step 1: Think about a recent situation where you felt stuck, overwhelmed, or reactive. Write down what happened, how you responded, and how you felt.

Step 2: Ask Yourself, "What do I believe about myself or my life that keeps me stuck?"

Example: "I believe I need to have everything figured out before I can start something new."

What if that belief isn't true? What more could you create if you didn't have to "figure it all out" first?

Step 3: Fear often keeps us from creating something new. Reflect on how caution and fear may have served you in the past (e.g., keeping you safe as a child). Then, consider how it might be limiting you now. What am I afraid might happen if I get out of my comfort zone?

Step 4: Many of our limitations come from old identities. How would life be different if I no longer carried the burden of my past?

Reactivity Awareness Journaling

Now it's time to build awareness around when and how reactivity shows up in daily life.

Step 1: For the next few days, keep a small journal or notebook with you. Whenever you notice yourself feeling triggered, overwhelmed, or reactive, take a moment to jot down:

The Situation: What happened?

Your Reaction: How did you respond emotionally or physically?

The Story: What belief or thought may have fueled your reaction?

Alternative Response: How could you have responded from a place of creativity, intention, or abundance?

Example:

Situation: My partner didn't answer my text for hours.

Reaction: I felt anxious and assumed they were avoiding me.

Story: "I must have done something wrong." or "They are being inconsiderate!"

Alternative Response: "Maybe they're busy, and it's not about me. I can focus on my own activities until they respond."

ROOTS OF REACTIVITY

To understand why we react the way we do as adults, we must look at the stories that were written in the earliest chapters of our lives. These stories—like *"I'm not safe"* or *"I'm not good enough"*—didn't come from nowhere. Our experiences wrote them, often during childhood, when our brains were most impressionable. These stories get scribed, unnoticed and unchallenged, into the subconscious.

As kids with newly developing minds, we use self-blame to make our world safe. Psychoanalyst Dr. Ronald Fairbairn wrote in his body of work, *"It is better to be a sinner ruled by God than to live in a world ruled by the devil." (TED,2023)* Translation? When bad things happen, it's easier for a child to think, *"This is my fault,"* than to face the terrifying idea that their parents might not provide safety. After all, if the people in charge of the juice boxes are unreliable, a child's whole world seems dangerous.

From a neuroscientific perspective, these reactivity patterns are deeply rooted in the brain. During childhood, the brain is like a sponge, absorbing everything around it and storing it directly into the subconscious. When faced with stress or trauma, our brain's alarm system kicks into overdrive. When activated for long periods of times, the alarm system gets stuck in a loop, creating a baseline of fear or hyper-vigilance, purely out of habit.

The part of the brain responsible for rational thinking and problem-solving develops later in life. This means that, as children, we don't have the tools to logically process what's happening to us. Instead, we internalize our experiences emotionally and often blame ourselves. Like I said before, you don't have to experience a traumatic childhood to develop unhealthy patterns of dealing with the world. For example:

- If a parent is emotionally unavailable, a child might think, *"There's something wrong with me; I'm not lovable."*

- If a caregiver is critical or harsh, the child might conclude, *"I'll never be good enough."*

These beliefs are stored in the subconscious mind and form the foundation of how we react to life's challenges later on. The fact that all of these childhood coping mechanisms are in your subconscious means, your not conscious of them.

The most insidious thing about these old stories is that they don't stay in the past. Instead, they sneak into our present, often in our closest relationships. This is because our brains are wired to seek familiarity, even when familiarity is painful. The brain's propensity for the familiar is to save energy. Two of the most familiar coping mechanisms that get carried into adulthood are:

I'm not safe:

- You might find yourself drawn to partners or friends who are emotionally unavailable or unpredictable, mirroring the dynamics of your childhood.

- You might avoid intimacy altogether, preferring to keep others at arm's length to protect yourself.

- You may over-control your environment, obsessively planning to avoid uncertainty.

I'm not good enough:

- You may overwork or overachieve, hoping that success will finally make you feel worthy.

- You might become a people-pleaser, bending over backward to gain approval from others.

- Alternatively, you might avoid trying altogether, fearing failure so much that you don't take risks.

Such deeply rooted patterns can create self-fulfilling prophecies. The more we react from a place of fear or inadequacy, the more we reinforce those beliefs, creating a cycle that's hard to break.

The good news is that you don't have to stay stuck in these patterns. The first step is awareness and recognizing them for what they are: remnants of a story you inherited, not a universal truth you have to live by. As Maya Angelou famously said, *"Do the best you can until you know better. Then, when you know better, do better."* Understanding the roots of your reactivity is the beginning.

Understanding the Roots of Reactivity

To move forward, we need to understand where our patterns begin. Let's explore how your early experiences turned limiting beliefs may be shaping your reactions today. Use these prompts in this exercise to dismantle the assumptions that underpin your limiting beliefs and reframe your thinking.

Step 1 Reflection: Consider your childhood environment and the messages you internalized. For each of the following prompts, write down your memories or impressions:

How did the adults in your life show love or approval?

What happened when you made mistakes?

Were you encouraged to express your feelings, or were they dismissed?

Step 2 Connect the Dots: Look at your current patterns of reactivity. How might they connect to your childhood experiences?

For example:

- "I avoid conflict because, as a child, disagreements always turned into fights."

- "I push myself to overachieve because I was praised for good grades and little else."

Step 3 Visualization: Imagine your younger self experiencing these moments. How might you comfort or reassure that beautiful little creature that is you?

Reframing Limiting Beliefs

What actions would you take if you realized the stories you've been believing about yourself are not inherently true?

What is the story I'm telling myself about why I can't have what I want?

- *Example:* "I'm too old to start something new."
- *Question:* What if age is irrelevant to possibility?

Am I reacting to what I think is true or to what is actually true?

- *Example:* "If I take this risk, I'll fail, and everyone will judge me."
- *Question:* If my limitations are illusions, what can I achieve now?

Insight: How often do you project outcomes based on fear rather than reality? What if the opposite of your feared outcome is just as likely—or even more likely?

Reparenting the Inner Child

Heal old wounds and soften reactive patterns by nurturing the inner child.

Step 1: Close your eyes and imagine yourself as a child at the age when you first remember feeling unsafe, unworthy, or the earliest fearful moment that you can recall. Visualize sitting beside this younger version of yourself. Write a short letter offering comfort and reassurance to that precious child.

Step 2 Prompt: *"Dear younger me, I know you feel [insert emotion] when [describe experience]. I want you to know that you are safe now, and you don't have to be affraid anymore. I am here for you."*

Step 3 Reflection: How did it feel to connect with your younger self? What beliefs might you be ready to release?

AN INVITATION TO LIBERATION

Creativity is the opposite of familiarity. The creative path isn't about achieving perfection or avoiding discomfort. Creativity happens when we get out of the comfort zone of old habits and tap into the source of limitless energy and wisdom; our soul. You can create a life that reflects your truest desires by questioning your assumptions and aligning with your higher self.

Imagine the freedom of waking up each day knowing you're no longer bound by limiting beliefs. Instead, you're guided by love, curiosity, and what brings you joy. How much energy would that free up for you? What would that feel like? (If you need to hit pause and write down your answers to these questions. I'll wait!)

When you take responsibility for creating your life, you're no longer at the mercy of fear or outdated narratives. You're no longer a victim. You start to see challenges as opportunities, mistakes as stepping stones, and your desires as valid guides. You realize that the life you've always wanted isn't something you stumble upon—it's something you have the power to design moment by moment.

Reactivity is what happens when those old stories call the shots. It feels like being stuck on the treadmill at the gym—running as fast as you can but never getting anywhere. When you're reactive, you're constantly putting out fires, meeting expectations, and avoiding rejection or failure. It's exhausting.

For example, maybe your partner makes an offhand comment, and instead of brushing it off, you spiral into self-doubt because it triggers an old subconscious belief like, *"I'm not enough."* Or maybe you avoid asking for a promotion at work because, deep down, you're afraid of being told, *"No, you're not qualified or educated enough."* Reactivity keeps you playing small, stuck in the loop of fear and scarcity.

Creativity, on the other hand, is a whole different ball game. When you live from the creative being you were designed to be, you stop reacting to life and start shaping it. Life is something you shape with intention. Living from the perspective of abundance, life happens for you. Challenges no longer feel like insurmountable obstacles but opportunities to grow. Decisions come from a place of clarity and purpose, not fear or avoidance. Your daily mindset is focused on what's possible rather than what could go wrong. This transformation brings a sense of empowerment, peace, and freedom to live authentically and design a life that truly reflects who you are.

It's like tending a garden. Living reactively means you spend all your time yanking weeds, worrying about pests and storms, or obsessing over how your flowers compare to your neighbor's. But living creatively? That's when you realize you can plant whatever you want. You choose the seeds, nurture the soil, water the plants, and grow a personal, regenerative oasis. This is your time to clear out the weeds that are choking out your soul. Dig into those old beliefs, shine some sunlight on them, and then choose what you want to grow next. Because the truth is, you've always had the power—you just needed to see it.

What Does Freedom Mean to You?

To live with intention, you must align with your personal definition of freedom. Liberation doesn't require fixing or filling a void—it comes from realizing that you are whole and complete as you are. From that place, what possibilities emerge? Use the steps below to uncover your unique path.

Step 1: What is the life I'm resisting, and why? Take a few notes below:

Example: You might resist leaving a job you dislike because of fear of financial insecurity. What are you resisting? The discomfort of uncertainty or maybe perceived loss of stability?

Insight: What if true security lies in embracing the unknown?

Step 2: Visualize a day in the life of your liberated self. How do you move, think, and create? What choices feel natural when you're not bound by fear or old stories? What would my life look like if I were truly free of all fear?

Step 3: If nothing were missing in my life right now, what would I create in this moment?

Freedom Visualization

Step 1: Close your eyes and take a few deep breaths. Imagine waking up tomorrow with complete freedom—no fear, no self-doubt, no limitations. Visualize how your day unfolds.

Step 2: Take a few moments to reflect and answer the following questions:

What do you spend your time doing today?

Who are you with, and how do you feel around them?

What will feel natural and joyful?

Optional: Sketch or write about this "free" version of yourself.

THE SHIFT

At the heart of reactivity is a mindset of lack: *"There's not enough time, love, or resources, and I have to fight for what I need."* Creativity thrives on abundance: *"There's more than enough, and I am worthy of it all."*

This shift is a transformative way of living. When you move from lack to abundance, you stop seeing life as a competition and start trusting that everything unfolds for your highest good. You begin to focus on what you have instead of what you don't. Decisions become easier because you trust yourself to handle whatever comes your way.

In the story about Sarah, this shift started small. When she set a boundary with her coworker, she wasn't just saying "no" to a project; she was saying "yes" to herself. Each small act of self-trust planted seeds of abundance, allowing her to create a life that felt more aligned with who she really was.

Shifting from Reactivity to Creativity

Creating from abundance allows you to reach your goals. With the following exercise, practice choosing creativity and abundance over reactivity and lack.

Step 1: Pause and reflect. Think about a situation where you recently reacted out of fear or scarcity. What might have changed if you approached it from a place of creativity and abundance instead?

Step 2: Rewrite the story in your head. Choose one belief you identified earlier and reframe it.

Step 3: Create an action step. Commit to one small action that aligns with your new belief. For example, set boundaries, take a creative risk, or say no without overexplaining.

Creativity Challenge

The following exercise will help you reinforce creative action over reactive behavior.

Step 1: For each of the next seven days choose one small, intentional action that disrupts old reactive habits.

Examples:

- If you tend to say "yes" out of guilt, practice saying "no" without explanation.
- If you feel stuck in routine, take a new route to work or try a new hobby.
- If you tend to avoid conflict, initiate an honest conversation.

Step 2: At the end of seven days reflect on the following questions:

What action did you take that was out of the norm for you?

How did taking this action make you feel?

What insights did you gain about your ability to choose differently?

BOTTOM LINE

Two forces shape whether we live in reactivity or creativity: the ego and the soul. The ego, formed in childhood, thrives on fear and security, keeping us tethered to old patterns of scarcity and self-doubt. It created the inner critic voice that says, *"Play it safe. Don't risk failing. You're not enough."*

The soul, on the other hand, is timeless. It connects us to love, abundance, and possibility. It's the quiet nudge that whispers, *"I'll show you how to soar!"* When we tune into the soul's wisdom, we shift from reacting to creating, from fear to trust, from lack to abundance.

Reactivity belongs to the ego. Creativity flows from the soul. Learning to navigate these forces is key to stepping into your power as the creator of your own life. The cage you've been living in? The door has been open the whole time. You don't have to earn your freedom; you simply have to notice the door, step through the opening, and start rewriting your story. You already have everything you need to succeed.

When you step into the role of creator, you stop waiting for permission to live fully. You don't need anyone to tell you you're good enough, smart enough, or deserving. You claim it for yourself.

Remember, **you** are the author of your own story. What will you create in the next chapter of your life?

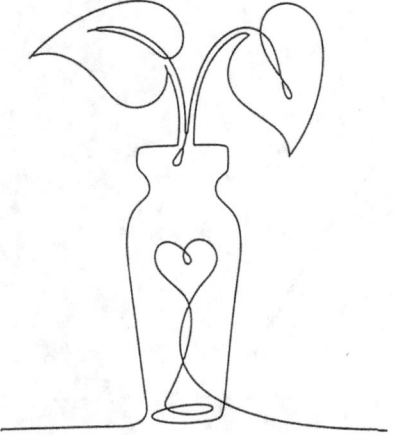

"You are imperfect, permanently and inevitably
flawed. And you are beautiful"

- Amy Bloom

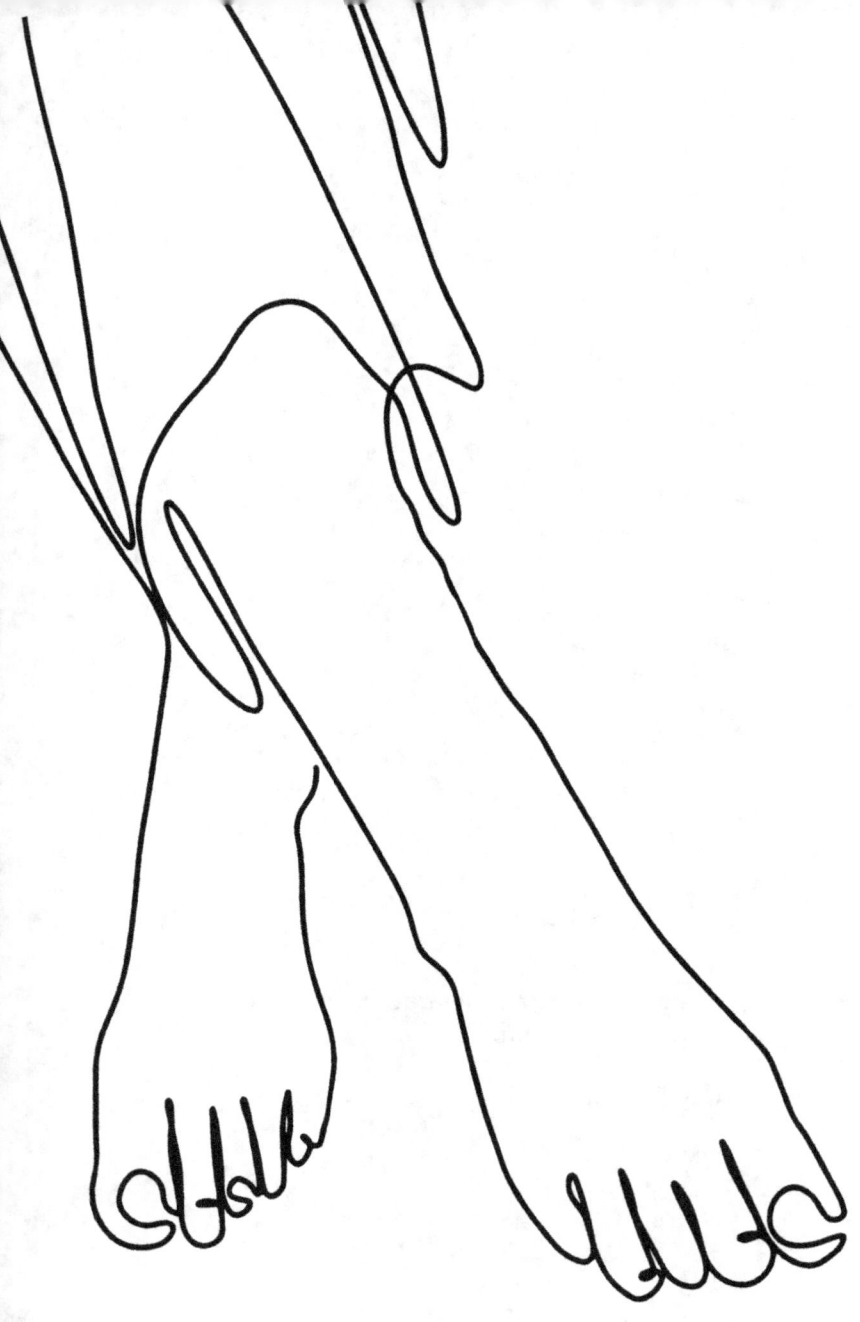

"Having compassion starts and ends with having compassion for all those unwanted parts of ourselves."

- Pema Chodron

Flourish After Fifty

05

Shake Off the Stickers

One of my favorite stories to read to my kids when they were little was *You Are Special* by Max Lucado. It's about a bunch of wooden people who go around slapping stickers on each other (kinda like social media, but without the filters and hashtags). The wooden people hand out stars for being excellent at something or just looking impressive and dots for being clumsy or 'not-so-great' at something.

The main character, Punchinello, had more dots than he could count and couldn't figure out how to get a single star. Then he met this amazing girl named Lucia, who had no stickers—none. Being stickerless was totally unheard of! Punchinello was dying to know how she pulled it off. When Punchinello asked Lucia about this she just shrugged and said she spent time with the guy who carved all the wooden people, and he told her she was valuable simply because she existed. She believed she was a perfect masterpiece, so the stickers didn't stick. People tried to put stickers on her but they just slid right off like she was made of Teflon.

THE COST OF CHASING APPROVAL

Lucia didn't need anyone else's opinion of her. She knew and accepted herself exactly the way she was created. How many times have you let someone else's opinion (good or bad) stick to you? In what areas of your life do you allow people or social expectations to define your direction? You may try to prove your worth by nailing your roles or piling up accomplishments. None of that external feedback is reliable. Not even a little bit. Your worth, my friend, comes from inside you.

The crazy thing is most of the time, you don't even realize you're betraying yourself. Remember the childhood coping mechanism used by the newly formed toddler brain in the chapter Free Your Mind? These behaviors were probably formed in early childhood. Like the 31 flavors of ice cream in a Baskin Robbins, the seeking of external validation or approval comes in many flavors. I've listed just a few. Which flavor is your go-to?

FLAVORS OF APPROVAL-SEEKING

Classic Overcommitment Sundae

A rich blend of saying yes when you mean no, topped with a generous dollop of people-pleasing.

Perfectionist Swirl

Made with the unrealistic expectation of flawlessness, leaving you exhausted but never satisfied.

Sorry Sorbet

A tangy mix of over-apologizing and taking responsibility for things that aren't your fault.

Conflict-Avoidance Crunch

A smooth base of staying silent, layered with chunks of unspoken opinions to keep the peace.

Compliment Cravings Cone

A sweet treat that keeps you fishing for reassurance, even when you already know you're enough.

Take-It-Personally Ripple

A bittersweet blend of overanalyzing and absorbing every offhand comment like it's about you.

Chameleon Cheesecake

Adapting your personality to fit the room—every room—until you're not sure who you are anymore.

Service-As-a-Shield Sundae

A deceptively sweet offering where serving others becomes a mask for people-pleasing. The motivation isn't love or compassion but fear of disappointing others or appearing selfish. True service nourishes; this flavor leaves you feeling hollow.

Work-Extra-Hard-for-Praise Pistachio

Packed with effort and topped with sprinkles of burnout, all for a crumb of validation

Permission-Seeking Parfait

Layer after layer of asking for advice or approval before making any decision.

Approval-By-Attire Gelato

An indulgent serving of dressing to impress, even when it doesn't feel authentic.

Needs-On-the-Back-Burner Nougat

Soft and chewy, this flavor melts your desires and feelings into the background to keep others happy.

Society's-Success Sundae

Topped with glittery but empty sprinkles of achievements defined by everyone but you.

Humor-Shift Sherbet

A zesty option where you change your jokes, speech, or opinions to match the crowd.

Social Media Validation Vanilla

Basic but addictive, this flavor craves likes, comments, and shares to feel worthy.

Imagine letting go of the worry and resentment that comes with pleasing others. If you didn't constantly chase validation, that energy could be used to explore passions, nurture relationships, and even practice deeper self-care. Every time you shed a fear-based belief, you reclaim a piece of your vitality, but that's not all. There's an added bonus to getting off this mental craving treadmill.

Recognize & Release Your Stickers

Step 1: Awareness

Reflect on a recent situation where you felt hurt, disappointed, or triggered by someone's opinion or judgment. Write it down. Then ask yourself:

What belief about myself did this situation reinforce?

Why did their words stick to me?

Step 2: Question the Belief

After reflecting on an incident, use the following template to explore the belief:

"I believed that _____ (e.g., I'm not smart enough, I always mess up)."

Is this belief absolutely true? Are you inadequate somehow?

Where did I learn this belief? Was it from my childhood, culture, or another person's projection?

Step 3: Reframe the Thought

Now, challenge the belief. Write down a new, empowering truth that replaces it. Revisit the new truths when old beliefs try to stick again.

Example: "I believed I am smart enough, resourceful enough, and capable enough regardless of what I once believed."

Approval-Seeking Ice Cream Menu

What is your personal favorite from the Approval Seeking Menu? This exercise will help you explore your favorite addictions!

Step 1: Review the *Flavors of Approval-Seeking* list from the chapter. Circle or highlight the "flavors" you recognize in yourself. Then, answer the following questions:

Which approval-seeking behavior do you most relate to?

How does this behavior show up in your life?

How does it make you feel?

What boundary or action could help you release this pattern?

What might it look like to release this behavior and prioritize self-approval?

SIMMERING IN RESENTMENT

I imagine you have heard the story about the frog in the pot of water? If you drop a frog into boiling water, it'll try to jump out immediately. But if you place it in lukewarm water and slowly turn up the heat, the frog doesn't realize it's in danger until it's too late. Much the same as the frog, when we seek validation from others and try to please them—at first, everything feels fine. Little by little, the temperature rises, and before you know it, you're simmering in resentment You say yes when you mean no, adjust your personality to fit the room, and tiptoe around your boundaries, thinking, *"It's just a little thing. No big deal."* Each time you silence your needs or desires to accommodate someone else, the water gets just a little hotter. You might not notice it at first—like that frog, it seems harmless enough. You think you're just being nice, but what you're really doing is slowly disconnecting from yourself and them. Boundaries give you the space to choose what aligns with your soul instead of letting the water boil.

Now, here's the tricky part. Most people-pleasers have this underlying hope that if they maintain the peace or put everyone else's needs before theirs, they'll be rewarded—someone will finally notice their effort, appreciate them, or return the sacrifice. When no one recognizes or acknowledges our sacrifice, frustration starts to bubble up. We begin to feel unappreciated, overlooked, or even taken for granted. All that effort, bending over backward for others, and what do you get in return? Nothing but a simmering pot of resentment.

It doesn't stop there. With the deep need for validation, you might keep piling on more tasks because you've convinced yourself that your worth is tied to how much you do for others. The heat in that pot rises, and soon you're burned out, exhausted, and—surprise!—even more resentful. Not only toward the people you're trying to please but also toward yourself for letting it go on. You're mad at them for not appreciating you, and you're mad at yourself for never saying no. It's a double whammy, no-win situation.

Then, one day, you wake up. You realize you don't even know who you are anymore. You've spent so much time twisting yourself into the mold you think others expect that you've lost touch with your own wants, needs, and desires. It's like the frog sitting in the boiling water, not realizing how bad things have gotten. When you lose yourself in the pursuit of approval, that disconnect feels like a slow suffocation.

People-pleasers tend to push these feelings down because they feel guilty about being angry or frustrated. It's easier to say, *"It's not a big deal,"* or *"I'm just trying to be kind,"* than to face the reality that you're starting to resent the very people you've been trying to please. But make no mistake—resentment doesn't disappear just because you ignore it. Left unchecked, it'll boil over, poisoning your relationships and your self-worth.

So, how do you cool the water down before it boils over? It starts with recognizing that you've been sitting in this pot for far too long. You have to acknowledge your own needs and stop seeking validation from others. Every time you say no, enforce a boundary, or speak up for yourself, you're turning the heat down, little by little.

The Power of "No"

This exercise aims to build self-worth by learning to prioritize your needs and setting healthy boundaries. Each time you set and maintain a boundary, you reclaim your energy and reinforce your sense of worth. Honoring your limits is a sign of self-respect. In the upcoming sections, we will explore the benefits of setting and maintaining boundaries.

Step 1: Identify Boundaries

List three recent situations where you said "yes" when you wanted to say "no." Reflect on why you agreed—were you trying to avoid conflict, seek approval, collect on a favor, or feel accepted?

1.

2.

3.

Step 2: The Cost of People-Pleasing

Write about how saying "yes" in each situation made you feel afterward. Did it lead to frustration or resentment? How did it affect your energy, time, or emotional well-being?

1.

2.

3.

Step 3: Practice Saying "No"

Choose a low-stakes scenario (e.g., declining an invitation or task that doesn't serve you). Practice saying "no" firmly and kindly. Write down the scenario and what happens afterward. How did it feel to prioritize yourself?

Step 4: Reflection

Setting boundaries is one thing. Enforcing them is another. Are you experiencing any guilt after enforcing boundaries?

RECLAIM YOUR ENERGY

No longer tolerating the nonsense that drains you is like slipping off a pair of stilettos after a long day. You feel relief. You feel calm, grounded, and maybe even a little giddy with the realization that your needs actually matter. Confidence replaces resentment, and you finally start to believe you deserve to take up space. And let's be honest—when was the last time you truly prioritized yourself without feeling guilty?

Boundaries, my friend, are your lifelines. Especially for midlife women who've spent decades bending over backward, juggling too many hats, and trying to keep everyone else afloat. Think of boundaries as the Teflon that keeps the stickers from sticking. They're the ultimate act of self-respect, protecting your energy, your peace, and your sanity from being trampled by the world's endless demands.

Setting boundaries isn't always a cakewalk. At first, it might feel like trying to say no to a pushy co-worker—it's awkward, uncomfortable, and guilt-inducing. You might worry you're being selfish or mean but you're not. That guilt? It's just old programming from years of being told your worth is tied to how much you do for others. Let the feelings and emotions bubble up, then watch them float away like a helium balloon.

The real magic happens when you start seeing boundaries as more than just lines—they're invitations. Invitations to say yes to yourself–to live authentically, to protect what matters, and to let go of what doesn't. You're validating your own needs, strengthening your self-worth, and creating space for joy, creativity, and maybe even the occasional nap.

So, let go of the guilt. Say no when you need to. Stop twisting yourself into a pretzel trying to make everyone else happy. When you honor your boundaries, you're reclaiming *you*. And isn't that worth it? I've included my favorite self-worth recipe below:

Recipe for Self-Worth

Ingredients:

- 1 cup of self-awareness (recognize where you feel drained or resentful)
- 2 tablespoons of clarified values (what matters most to you)
- A pinch of courage (start small and manageable)
- A generous sprinkle of kind, clear communication
- 1 heaping tablespoon of consistency (for pushback)
- A dollop of self-compassion (as needed)

Instructions:

Preheat Your Awareness:

Begin by noticing the moments in your day when you feel irritated, exhausted, or taken for granted. These feelings are like warning lights, signaling where your boundaries may need reinforcement.

Example: Do you dread answering texts from a particular person? Say yes to tasks out of guilt? These situations are ripe for the practice of enforcing boundaries.

Clarify Your Needs and Values:

Take some time to reflect on what makes you feel supported, energized, and respected. Jot down your non-negotiables—these are your guiding principles for setting boundaries.

Pro Tip: Boundaries are personal, so focus on what aligns with your priorities, not what others expect.

Start with Small Steps:

Think of boundaries as a recipe you're perfecting. Start with minor adjustments—like saying no to a small request that doesn't fit your schedule.

Example: Instead of agreeing to a last-minute coffee date when you're already stretched thin, politely decline and suggest another time.

Mix in Clear, Kind Communication:

Combine directness with compassion when expressing your boundaries.

Script Suggestions:

"I can't take on that project right now, but I hope you find the help you need."

"I need some quiet time after work to recharge. Let's catch up later."

Pro Tip: Keep it simple. You don't owe anyone a lengthy explanation.

Prepare for Pushback:

Not everyone will applaud your new boundaries, especially if they've benefited from your lack of them. Stir in consistency—practice holding the line, even when others challenge it.

> **Reminder: Setting boundaries is more about retraining yourself than it is about retraining others.**

Fold in Self-Compassion:

If boundary-setting feels awkward or guilt-inducing, add a healthy dollop of self-compassion. Remind yourself that prioritizing your well-being isn't selfish—it's essential. Like any skill, it takes practice to master.

WHEN TO USE THIS RECIPE:

- When you feel resentful, overwhelmed, or emotionally drained.

- When you find yourself dodging certain people or situations.

- When you're always the go-to person and feel exhausted but unable to say no.

- When your goals and priorities have been sidelined to meet others' demands.

Serving Suggestion:

This recipe for self-worth is versatile. It cooks up boundaries like the ones served at the Boundary Bistro, where the dishes are carefully crafted to nourish your soul, restore your energy, and empower you to show up authentically. Unlike the flavors of people-pleasing that leave you drained and resentful, this menu features wholesome, satisfying options designed to help you say no with confidence, protect your peace, and reclaim your life. Don't worry—frog is not on the menu. Take a look at the offerings and see which dishes you'd like to savor as you cultivate a life that truly nourishes you.

Appetizers

"No, Thank You" Nachos

Crispy chips of clarity topped with the cheese of firm decisions, a sprinkle of polite refusal, and a side of guilt-free salsa. Perfect for practicing small but powerful boundaries.

Pause-and-Breathe Bruschetta

Fresh slices of mindfulness served with a spread of thoughtful pauses to give yourself space before committing to anything.

Entrees

The Respect-My-Time Risotto

A creamy, perfectly balanced dish made with chunks of "my time is valuable" and seasoned with clear start-and-end times for commitments.

Energy Preservation Platter

A hearty serving of priorities, with sides of limited emotional labor and an extra helping of "I can't do that right now, but thank you for understanding."

Authenticity Alfredo

Rich and satisfying, this dish celebrates being yourself, unapologetically. Served with a drizzle of self-expression and a sprinkle of saying no to fit-in behaviors.

Boundary Buddha Bowl

A nourishing mix of healthy limits, self-care practices, and unapologetic "nos," all tossed in a dressing of self-respect.

Sides

Silent Mode Sweet Potatoes

Perfect for turning off notifications and reclaiming your downtime.

Non-Negotiable Naan

Warm and soft, but firm in its stance to protect your self-care rituals and time for yourself.

Desserts

"That's Not My Problem" Pie

A light and liberating slice made with layers of letting go and topped with a dollop of responsibility only for what's yours.

Guilt-Free Gelato

A creamy, indulgent dessert made with self-compassion and sprinkled with the freedom of living life on your own terms.

The dishes on this menu were created to satisfy your appetite for wholeness, trim down the excess and nourish your values. Each time you honor your needs, you're reminding yourself—and the world—that your worth isn't determined by anyone else's stars or dots. So, choose from this menu of boundaries, and let each decision you make be a loving step toward the flourishing life you were carved to live. Bon appétit.

Boundary Bingo

Step 1: Complete at least four boundary-setting actions in a row (horizontally, vertically, or diagonally). Some rows are easier to complete than others.

Say No Without Explanation	Take a Guilt-Free Break	Set a Clear Work Limit	Prioritize Self-Care & Health
Cancel a Plan You Didn't Want to Do Anyway	Ask for Help Without Guilt	Walk Away from a Negative Conversation	Politely Deny Giving a Favor
Call in a Mutually Understood Favor	Go on Vacation	Say Yes to Something You Really Want But Others Discourage	Buy Something You've Always Wanted
Empower Your Kids by Saying No to Dependent Asks	Stand Your Ground and Have Uniterupted Quiet Time	Reject an Unhealthy Habit (we often cross our own boundries)	Set the Rules of a New Relationship

Ground Yourself In The Now

This exercise aims to shift from seeking approval in the past or future to anchoring your self-worth in the present moment. This practice roots you in the present, where your self-worth isn't tied to past beliefs, mistakes, roles, or future anxieties. Being present helps you realize that your value exists independently of anyone else's opinion.

Step 1: Mindful Breath Awareness

Sit in a quiet space and close your eyes. Focus on your breath, feeling each inhale and exhale fully. Allow yourself to become grounded in the present moment. Take five deep breaths and repeat an affirmation that resonates with you.

Example: "I am enough right now."

Step 2: Release Past Attachments

Reflect on a recent situation where you sought approval or validation. Write it down on seperate paper. Now, consciously release it. You might even want to physically get rid of the paper by throwing it away, burning it, or throwing it in the ocean.

On a blank sheet of paper, write:

"I release the need for approval from _____ (the person or situation). I am enough, exactly as I am."

Step 3: Daily Mindfulness Practice

Commit to 5 minutes of mindful breathing each morning for the next week. Each time your mind drifts to thoughts of approval or judgment, gently bring it back to the present moment, repeating, "I am enough."

BOTTOM LINE

Lucia from *You Are Special* taught us that when we know our worth, the stickers—both stars and dots—can't stick. True self-worth doesn't come from outside of you it comes from your soul. It comes from embracing who you are and valuing yourself simply because you exist.

Chasing validation and people-pleasing may feel safe in the moment, but they only lead to exhaustion, resentment, and a disconnection from your true self. Boundaries are your way back to you. When you honor your boundaries, you stop twisting yourself into shapes that don't fit and start living a life that's uniquely yours. Every "no" to something misaligned becomes a "yes" to your soul. You reclaim your time, reinforce your worth, and create space for joy, creativity, and deeper connections.

So, let go of the guilt. Choose boundaries over burnout. The stickers can only stick if you let them. You, my friend, were carved for a life of freedom, authenticity, and flourishing. Step into it boldly—you're worth it.

The next step in this journey is facing fears head-on. It's time to turn on the light and look under the bed to take a look at the proverbial monster lurking there. Only by confronting the shadowy things can we free ourselves to live with authenticity, courage, and unshakable self-worth.

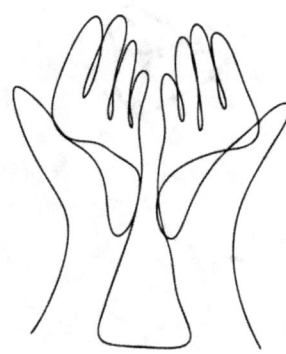

"One is a great deal less anxious if one feels perfectly free to be anxious, and the same may be said of guilt."

- Alan Watts

"Until you make the unconscious conscious, it will direct your life, and you will call it fate."

- Carl Jung

06

CHAPTER SIX

Facing the Monster Under the Bed

D o you remember being afraid of the dark as a kid? I used to be terrified of monsters under my bed. My imagination started running wild as soon as my parents turned out the lights. The house got quiet, and the only sounds were the soft hum of the refrigerator and the faint sound of a dog barking in the distance. Tucked in bed, all cozy under the blankets, I did not feel safe. My eyes were WIIIIIIDE open, and my heart raced. Why? Because I knew there was a monster under the bed. I didn't think—I knew as sure as Saturday morning cartoons something was lurking in the darkness under the bed.

My parents told me a hundred times, "There's no such thing as monsters." However, at that moment, in the dark, under the covers, I wasn't buying it. I was convinced that something would grab me the second I let my big toe hang over the edge. Every creak in the house became proof the end was near. The only thing that would calm my nerves was turning on the light.

I took a deep breath, wiggled out of the covers, and perched at the edge of the bed like a cat ready to pounce. Summoning all the courage my six-year-old self could muster, I launched myself across the room to the light switch. Heart racing, I flipped on the light—and then. Nothing. No claws, no growls—just the muffled steady hum of the refrigerator and the pounding of my heart. With a flick of a switch, the monster wasn't so monstrous anymore. Nothing was under the bed but a few stray socks collecting dust bunnies. As children, the monster under the bed seemed real enough to keep us up at night. Eventually, we learned to flip on the light, peek underneath the bed, and find nothing. That reassurance helped us sleep, made us feel safe, and allowed us to conquer one of our earliest fears.

MEET YOUR SHADOW SIDE

As adults, the monsters haven't disappeared—they've just gone deeper, hiding in the shadows of our subconscious. These fears no longer take the form of something under the bed; instead, they operate in the shadow of the the subconscious, disguised as busyness, procrastination, perfectionism, or even cynicism. They whisper doubts like, *"Am I still relevant?"* or *"Why did my marriage fail?"* and keep us trapped in patterns that limit our growth. Much like the imagined monsters of childhood, these shadowy fears grow stronger in the dark, feeding on avoidance and denial.

The good news is the same courage it took to flip on the light as a child still lives in us today. By shining a light on our shadows—those hidden fears and limiting beliefs—we can finally see them for what they are: illusions that no longer serve us. Facing these parts of ourselves head-on allows us to dissolve their grip and step into a life of freedom, transformation, and authenticity.

What are these monsters really? Some of them are the parts of ourselves we've been hiding. The parts we refuse to look at, the parts we keep in the dark—our shadow side. Psychologists describe the shadow as the unconscious part of our personality, made up of the traits and emotions we suppress because we fear they might be unacceptable. It's the part of ourselves we've rejected in order to fit in, gain approval, or avoid pain.

When you stop and think about why your co-worker upset you, dig below the surface. Adult fears often stem from a voice in your mind tied to a subconscious belief operating just below the surface. This belief perpetuates feelings of unworthiness or fearfulness because of previous experiences. For example:

- **"I'm only loveable if I achieve."** A child praised solely for accomplishments might grow into an adult who suppresses rest or creativity, believing their worth is conditional.

- **"Expressing anger makes me a bad person."** A child punished for showing anger might bury it in their shadow, leading to a fear of confrontation or vulnerability.

- **"My needs make me selfish."** A child labeled "too needy" might suppress their desires, believing their value lies in serving others at the expense of themselves.

Our fears, and the parts of ourselves they conceal, aren't enemies to be defeated. They are mirrors, revealing where love is withheld.

Unconditional love for ourselves doesn't cling to the good and reject the bad. It embraces the fullness of who we are—the brilliant and the messy parts together. Love that is conditional on being good or worthy is not love. It's a transaction. Real love is transformative. It says, *"I see your fears, your mistakes, your anger, and your insecurities, and I love you anyway. Not despite them, but because they're part of you."*

When we extend this profound acceptance to ourselves, we create a space where all parts of us are welcome. Self-love becomes an act of integration, a declaration that the whole of our existence is loveable. Loving ourselves means we no longer see our shadow as a flaw to fix but as a teacher, a source of wisdom and strength. It allows us to grow, not by erasing our perceived bad parts but by embracing the beautiful complexity of our humanity.

Explore Shadow Archetypes

By identifying shadow archetypes, you will gain insight into how they shape your thoughts and actions. This will allow you to bring them into the light and integrate their hidden strengths. The five most common are listed below.

The Wounded Child

Traits: Feelings of unworthiness, insecurity, and fear of abandonment.

Root Causes: Often tied to childhood experiences of neglect, criticism, or unmet emotional needs.

Signs: You might constantly seek approval, fear rejection, or feel stuck in a victim mentality.

Hidden Gift: The Wounded Child can teach empathy, resilience, and the importance of nurturing yourself and others.

The Inner Critic

Traits: Self-judgment, perfectionism, and harsh internal dialogue.

Root Causes: Developed as a way to meet high standards or avoid failure.

Signs: Overthinking, procrastination, or feeling "never good enough."

Hidden Gift: The Inner Critic can become a discerning voice, helping you strive for growth without self-sabotage.

The Rebel

Traits: Defiance, anger toward authority, and resistance to rules or expectations.

Root Causes: Often stems from feeling controlled, misunderstood, or powerless.

Signs: Difficulty with authority figures or sabotaging situations where compromise is needed.

Hidden Gift: The Rebel can inspire creativity, individuality, and the courage to challenge the status quo.

The Caretaker

Traits: Over-responsibility, putting others' needs first, and difficulty saying no.

Root Causes: This may arise from a desire to feel needed or to avoid feelings of selfishness.

Signs: Burnout, resentment, or losing touch with your own needs.

Hidden Gift: The Caretaker can guide you toward healthy compassion and the ability to foster meaningful connections.

The Saboteur

Traits: Self-sabotage, procrastination, and fear of success.

Root Causes: Often rooted in fear of change or unworthiness.

Signs: Abandoning goals, staying in unhealthy situations, or downplaying achievements.

Hidden Gift: The Saboteur can help uncover where you need to address fears and strengthen self-trust.

> **By working with these archetypes rather than rejecting them, you will gain the tools to embrace your shadow and move toward greater wholeness.**

Step 1: Write down a reoccurring fear or thought.

Example: "I always feel like I'll mess things up if I take on something new."

Step 2: Which archetype does this thought reflect?

Example: This reflects *The Saboteur,* tied to a fear of failure and a belief that I'm not good enough.

Step 3: Ask yourself, "How does it help me?"

Example: It has kept me feeling safe, protecting me from overwhelming risks. It's made me cautious and thoughtful in planning my actions.

Step 4: Ask yourself, "How does the shadow archetype hinder me?

Example: It's held me back from pursuing opportunities that could bring growth and fulfillment. I've avoided taking risks, keeping me stuck and unfulfilled.

Step 5: How I Can Integrate This Archetype?

Example: Recognize that my Saboteur isn't trying to hurt me but to protect me from failure. Reframe its message by saying, "It's okay to take risks; even if I fail, I'll learn and grow." Take small, manageable steps to build trust in my ability to handle challenges.

EXPOSING THE SHADOW

Imagine a life where you're less reactive and more centered—where the slights that once sent you into a spiral now roll off your back like water off a duck's back. By integrating your shadow, you reclaim pieces of yourself you forgot were there, empowering you to live your best life.

The same stories that keep us trapped in cycles of reactivity, like people-pleasing, come from the same beliefs we explored in the chapter Free Your Mind—"*I'm not good enough, I'm not safe,*" etc. To truly expose what's lurking in the shadow, we need to understand how it works in tandem with another key part of our psyche—the ego. These two forces, often at odds, are deeply interconnected. Their push and pull shapes how we view ourselves and interact with the world, making their relationship essential to letting go of what no longer works.

To understand the shadow fully, let's explore its relationship with the ego—the part of us that defines our sense of identity. The shadow is the hidden closet called the subconscious, where we store the parts of ourselves we don't want to face. It thrives in judgment and shame. The ego is the diligent gatekeeper standing at the door, banishing any part of you that is not acceptable. Now, the ego is just trying to keep us presentable so we can move through the world without any issues. Ironic, isn't it! What if we offered understanding to those undesirable parts instead of rejection?

Rather than labeling parts of yourself as inadequate or unworthy, recognize them as chapters in the story of your life. Your mistakes, fears, and even failures are not flaws; they're evidence of your growth and humanity. Many traits you've buried as "negative" often have a hidden gift. Stubbornness can be a mask for perseverance. Sensitivity, dismissed as weakness, can be the wellspring of empathy and connection. By reframing these aspects, you can see the shadow not as a flaw but as an integral part of your wholeness.

The ego's protective nature can create blind spots. When the ego is overly invested in maintaining a specific image—of being strong, kind, successful, or unflawed—it actively suppresses anything that might threaten that narrative. This suppression creates the shadow.

For example:

- If the ego identifies as "generous," it may suppress feelings of resentment or selfishness, relegating them to the shadow.

- If the ego clings to being "stoic," it might bury vulnerability or sensitivity.

- If the ego defines itself as "hardworking," it may reject rest or playfulness, labeling it laziness or frivolousness.

In this way, the ego and the shadow are two sides of the same coin. The more rigid the ego adheres to its identity, the larger its shadow casts.

The shadow protects the ego but at a cost. Ironically, the shadow forms as a way to support the ego's desire for stability and acceptance. By hiding what the ego fears, the shadow helps preserve the identity we project to the world. The more we suppress parts of ourselves, the more fragmented we feel internally.

This inner fragmentation can manifest as:

Projection: We see in others what we cannot accept in ourselves. For instance, if our ego refuses to acknowledge anger, we might become hyper-aware of and critical of others' anger.

Emotional Reactivity: Shadowy aspects we've buried tend to surface in unexpected ways, often triggered by stress or conflict. These reactions feel disproportionate because they stem from unresolved internal tensions.

Self-sabotage: Suppressed parts of us don't disappear; they find indirect ways to express themselves, such as procrastination, avoidance, or destructive habits.

The key to personal growth doesn't mean dismissing the ego or dissolving the shadow—it involves creating a harmonious relationship between the two. Embracing the connection between the ego and shadow transforms how we view ourselves. No longer at war with our perceived flaws, we step into the freedom of self-acceptance, where the light and the dark coexist in perfect balance.

Here's how:

Expand the Ego's Narrative: Instead of clinging to a narrow definition of who we are, we can invite the ego to hold a broader, more inclusive identity. For example, "I can be strong and vulnerable" or "I can be generous and still have needs." This softens the ego's defenses and allows space for shadow integration.

See the shadow as a Teacher: When shadowy aspects come up—whether in the form of projections or strong emotions—we can approach them with curiosity rather than judgment. What is this reaction trying to show me about myself?

Practice Compassion for Both Sides: The ego works hard to protect us, and the shadow holds the parts of us that long to be seen. Both deserve compassion. By embracing this duality instead of ignoring it, we move closer to wholeness.

"A mind committed to compassion is like an overflowing reservoir - a constant source of energy, determination and kindness."

- THE DALAI LAMA

Meet Your Monsters

This activity is designed to help you identify, confront, and transform the emotional fears and doubts that may be holding you back. By recognizing fear and merely observing it, you can diminish its power, build resilience, and empower yourself.

Step 1: Reflect on the emotional fears and doubts lurking in the shadows. These could be fears related to change, self-doubt, or feeling the pressure to meet expectations; anything that might be holding you back. Think about the hidden part of yourself that fear might be protecting or hiding. Is there a fear of failure, a suppressed desire for creativity or freedom? Write down three "emotional monsters" you've identified.

Monster 1:

Monster 2:

Monster 3:

Step 2: For each emotional monster, describe how it has affected your life. Consider how it has influenced your decisions, limited your actions, or impacted your overall well-being. Reflect on the possible root cause of the fear or anxiety. Is there anything from childhood that might be causing it?

How Monster 1 affects me:

How Monster 2 affects me:

How Monster 3 affects me:

Step 3: It's time to flip the switch and shine a light on these monsters. For each one, write down a positive action you can take to confront it. This could be a small step toward facing the fear or a change in perspective that helps you see the situation differently.

Monster 1 Action Step:

Monster 2 Action Step:

Monster 3 Action Step:

Step 4: Reframe each emotional monster in a way that diminishes its power over you. For example, if your fear is, *"It's not safe to be me,"* reframe it as *"My authenticity is my power and my peace..."* Write down these new, empowering perspectives.

Monster 1 New Perspective:

Monster 2 New Perspective:

Monster 3 New Perspective:

Step 5: Take action. Choose one small action from your list that you can take today or this week to start confronting one of your emotional monsters. Write down the action and commit to doing it.

Action:

Date to Complete:

Step 6: Reflect and review. After taking your action, reflect on the experience. Use the space below to write about your experience and any new insights.

How did confronting your fear feel?

What did you learn about yourself?

How can you continue to apply this process to other emotional challenges?

Mapping Your Emotions with Color

Art can bypass the analytical mind and access deeper parts of ourselves that are harder to express. When we experience fear, stress, or suppressed emotions, these feelings often live in specific parts of our body. Using color as a tool, we can map these sensations, giving them a shape and a voice and allowing us to process them in a nonverbal and intuitive way.

Use color and art to visually explore where emotions, fears, and shadow traits show up in your body. This exercise engages your creativity to connect with emotions that may be difficult to articulate with words.

Please Note: This activity doesn't require artistic skill—it only requires that you listen to your body and use color to indicate what it's telling you. Try associating color with different parts of your body.

Materials Needed:

- Colored pencils, crayons, pastels, or markers.
- A quiet space and 10-15 minutes of uninterrupted time.

Step 1: To calm the mind and let go of the outside world, close your eyes, take a few deep breaths and sit quietly for a few moments. Set the intention to tune into your body with curiosity and compassion.

Step 2: Starting from the top of your head and moving down to your feet, notice any sensations in your body. Pay attention to areas that feel tight, heavy, warm, cold, tense, tingly, or even numb. Any sensation. Don't judge or try to change these sensations—observe them.

Step 3: In the space provided, draw an outline of a human body or any shape that comes to mind. Next, assign a color to represent each emotion or sensation you feel. Trust your instincts. There is no wrong way to choose colors. If it helps create a key.

For example: Red for anger or tension, Blue for sadness or heaviness, Yellow for nervous energy or restlessness, Black or gray for fear or suppressed emotions, Green for calm or release, Purple for joy.

Drawing space:

Step 4: By mapping your sensations with color, you can honor the messages your body sends and release fear or suppressed emotions creatively and gently.

Tip: Revisit this exercise whenever you feel stuck or overwhelmed. Mapping emotions can reveal patterns over time and provide a powerful tool for healing and self-discovery.

Once you've finished your emotional body map, take a moment to look at what you created. Ask yourself:

What emotions or fears am I holding onto, and where are they showing up?

Is there a pattern? Do certain areas tend to hold tension or heaviness more than others?

Write a few sentences about what your map reveals.

LETTING THE SOUL SHINE

The soul (the authentic part of you) remains untouched by the ego and the shadow. It is like a brilliant light bulb that's been covered with dust. It's inherently radiant, a unique expression of light and love, but its brilliance often gets dimmed by the unexamined tension between the ego and the shadow. While sometimes seen as obstacles to overcome, the two parts of the psyche are essential allies in the journey toward wholeness. When integrated, they act as catalysts, allowing the soul's light to shine and empowering you to flourish in life.

And really, is there a better time than midlife to tackle this? After all, the very word *menopause* seems to hold a wickedly hidden message: it's time to *pause*. It's nature's not-so-subtle way of handing you a flashing neon sign that says, *"Slow down, reflect, and recalibrate."* With the hormonal shifts opening the floodgates on raw emotions and old stories, midlife offers the perfect opportunity to highlight shadow work and clear the cobwebs from under the bed you've been lying on all these years. After all, the mood swings and insomnia might as well have a purpose, right?

Midlife may come with hot flashes and night sweats, but it's also a fire that burns away what no longer serves you (literally and figuratively). Working through the ego-shadow tension fuels transformation. When the ego and shadow are integrated, they create a clear channel for the soul to shine, making this chapter of life one of unparalleled radiance and empowerment.

Here's how.....

To live authentically, we must bring the entirety of who we are into the light. This includes our successes and strengths and our perceived flaws, mistakes, and contradictions. Self-love doesn't curate a perfect image of ourselves; it highlights the truth of our complexity and says, *"This is me."*

The shadow holds hidden gifts. Within the parts of ourselves we've exiled lie dormant treasures. That suppressed anger, once acknowledged, can become the fire that fuels healthy boundaries and self-respect.

Vulnerability, once feared, can deepen your relationships and cultivate genuine connection. Even traits like selfishness, when understood, might reveal the self-care you've been neglecting.

By embracing the shadow, we reclaim the pieces of ourselves and unlock the strengths and wisdom waiting in the wings.

Integrating the shadow heals the shame we've buried for so long. Many elements of the shadow are tied to shame—the belief that we are fundamentally flawed. Facing the shadow allows us to dismantle these old stories. When we bring shame into the light, it can no longer control us. We reclaim our worthiness—not because we're perfect but because we are human.

Meet Your Future Self

This exercise connects you to the most authentic, courageous version of yourself. By visualizing your future self and hearing the encouragement, you're reminded that the life you want is possible—and that the choices you make today shape the person you are tomorrow.

Create a vision, a manifesto, for the life you want to live and reconnect with your true nature as you move forward. Keep the letter close and read it from time to time as you move forward. It's more than a vision; it's a promise to yourself. One year from now, you'll look back and see just how far you've come.

Step 1: Meet Your Future Self. Sit somewhere peaceful where you won't be interrupted. Take a few deep breaths, and allow yourself to settle into the present moment. Close your eyes and imagine your life one year from now. Picture yourself having worked through the fears, beliefs, and patterns that once held you back. See yourself living in alignment with your core values—joyful, confident, and free.

What does this version of you look like?

Where are you?

What are you doing? Who are you with?

How do you feel?

Step 2: On a separate sheet of paper, write a letter to your present self as if it's coming from this future version of you. Share your wisdom, encouragement, and insights. Let your future self remind you of the strength, courage, and resilience that got you here.

Use prompts like:

- Dear [Your Name], I want you to know that...

- You were afraid of [insert fear], but here's what happened when you faced it...

- "This is what I've learned about life, love, and joy...

- Keep going because...

Step 3: When you're done, fold up the letter, put it in an envelope, and write "Open one year from today" on the front. Keep it somewhere safe, or give it to a trusted friend to hold for you.

Step 4: Next, write down 2-3 small actions you can take *now* to move toward the life your future self described. These don't have to be big leaps—small, intentional steps are better.

Example Actions:

- "I will say no to one thing this week that doesn't align with my values."

- "I will speak up in the next meeting, even if I feel nervous."

- "I will take 10 minutes each morning to practice mindfulness."

Light Up the Shadow Visualization

For this exercise you will need to find a quiet spot where there are no interruptions. Visualization is a form of meditation. This visualization will focus on bringing compassion and healing to suppressed parts of the self. It may be helpful to turn on some relaxing music or nature sounds.

Step 1: Close your eyes and visualize holding a lantern in a dark room. Walk toward a shadowy figure (your suppressed emotion or trait). Shine the light on it and observe. What does it look like? What is it feeling? Ask: "What do you need from me?" Afterward, write about the experience.

Step 2: Answer the following reflection questions:

What did you learn about your shadow?

How did it feel to bring light to this part of yourself?

Shadow Work

This exercise will guide you through identifying suppressed traits, exploring their hidden gifts, and offering your shadow the compassion it deserves. When we stop resisting the shadow, it becomes a source of power, not shame.

Step 1: Write about a trait or emotion you avoid showing, such as anger, assertiveness, or vulnerability.

Reflect on the following questions:

- What are the traits or emotions I avoid showing?

- When was the first time I was taught this trait was bad or unacceptable?

- What happens when I suppress this trait? How does it show up in my fears, relationships, or decisions?

Step 2: Discover the gift in the shadow. Every shadow trait has a hidden strength. Reflect on the positive aspects of the trait you suppress.

Example: "My assertiveness could help me set boundaries and honor my needs without guilt.

What strength or wisdom could this trait offer me if I expressed it in a healthy way?

If I embrace this part of me, how can it help me move past fear and live more authentically?

Step 3: For this step, choose from two different exercises. The objective is to extract a new understanding of your shadow side and its connection to your fears.

Choose one of the following:

A. Practice self-acceptance and compassion. Write a letter to your shadow self, acknowledging and accepting it as part of you. Use kind, compassionate language.

B. An alternative to writing a letter to the shadow would be a meditation exercise. Find a quiet and comfortable spot where you will not be disturbed. Close your eyes and take a few deep breaths. Then, in your mind's eye, open yourself up to meeting your shadow. Don't be afraid to ask questions and express emotions. Then, write down any new insights.

BOTTOM LINE

When we extend love to our shadow, we take a profound step toward self-acceptance, bringing together our fractured parts. This act of integration transforms how we see ourselves and the world. No longer driven by the need to be perfect, we embrace the truth of our humanity.

Much like flipping on the light to face the childhood monster under the bed, shadow work reveals that what we feared was never as terrifying as it seemed. The shadow isn't an enemy but a guide, waiting to show us the depths of our strength and the beauty of our imperfections. By embracing this truth, we rest in the awareness of who we are—a complex tapestry of light and shadow, strength and vulnerability. In that acceptance, we find peace and wholeness. This kind of transformation doesn't just create a ripple in your life; it creates a shock wave.

The monster under the bed doesn't disappear when the light is turned on—it transforms. What once terrified us becomes a teacher, a guide, and ultimately, a part of who we are. Facing that monster isn't the end of the journey. It's the beginning of living with open eyes and open hearts—no longer afraid of the dark but embracing it as part of the light.

"What's the greatest lesson a woman should learn? That since day one, she's already had everything she needs within herself. It's the world that convinces her she did not."

- ALISA VITTI

"You cannot stop the waves, but you can learn to surf."

- Jon Kabat-Zinn

Flourish After Fifty

07

CHAPTER SEVEN

Waves of Emotion

M y husband and I recently committed to a significant lifestyle change—we'd gone vegan, embracing whole-food, plant-based dishes with fresh ingredients. We got into a nice healthy routine: eating right, exercising, and feeling great—then—BOOM—chaos.

The evening was typical in terms of weather for late May. The air was light and cool, and a gentle breeze rustled the tree tops. Leaving the restaurant, my husband and I walked to our car, chatting with friends. On the drive home, feeling happy and content, we talked about all the home projects we accomplished this spring. We both felt ready to settle into a calm and relaxing summer, spending lots of time reading by the backyard pool and cooking yummy vegan dishes with the fresh produce from our newly planted garden.

At about 2:30 a.m., we woke to storm sirens and the roar of a tornado plowing through our property. From the safety of the basement, I heard the howling winds rearranging heavy metal chairs on the covered deck above and the crackling sound of trees breaking like match sticks. Then, I felt a heavy, dull, ground-shaking shutter rattle my home to its bones. At first light, we emerged to see mature oak trees (91 feet tall) covering our home, cars, and outbuildings. Of course, the power went out, leaving us without electricity. Adding to the devastation, the public electrical lines fell across our driveway, trapping us on our property. Cleaning up the debris and getting tarps over the gaping holes in our roof to prevent further water damage took three exhausting days.

During this time, I was freaking out inside. My internal world was mirroring my external world. The stress of the situation made me want to abandon my new, healthy eating habits and eat anything in sight—preferably something comforting (think childhood favorites). After all, who wouldn't want to dive into a comforting bowl of mac and cheese or crawl back into bed with a handful of warm chocolate chip cookies?

My brain went into pure reactivity. The inner critic (voice of the ego) chimed in: *"Screw your new healthy diet. All of your energy needs to go into fixing and repairing this mess. You don't have the mental capacity to think about what and how you need to eat. Grab whatever is available and keep moving. There are more important things to think about."* Then I paused and took a few deep breaths while I took note of how my body felt under all that stress.

I was trying to use food to comfort myself, to escape the feeling of fear and anxiety. My old habits of dealing with stress were trying to creep back into my life. I sat quietly with myself for a moment and asked, *"What do I really need?"* It turned out it wasn't comfort food. It was calm, clarity, and compassion. Fueling my body with healthy, vibrant food would help, not hurt me, in this situation. In short, I needed to love myself through this stress-filled situation instead of letting the situation control me.

FEELINGS VS. EMOTIONS

Ever feel like you're drowning in your own emotions, only to realize you're actually treading water in a sea of feelings? You're not alone—and you're not crazy. People often use the terms "emotions" and "feelings" interchangeably. They are not the same. Think of emotions as the waves themselves and feelings as the stories we tell about those waves.

Emotions are like pop-up ads on the internet—fast, uninvited, and often a little startling. They're your body's immediate response to something happening around or inside you. Fear when you hear a loud noise? That's your survival instinct kicking in. Joy when you hear your favorite song? That's your body saying, *"This is great! Do more of this."* Emotions are universal and hardwired into our biology.

Feelings, however, are where things get complicated. They're your mind's interpretation of those emotions, filtered through the lens of your thoughts, beliefs, and life experiences. They're like the comments section under a social media post—they can turn a simple message into a full-blown drama. For instance:

The emotion of *fear* might feel like anxiety if you're imagining the worst-case scenario for an upcoming challenge.

The emotion of *sadness* might feel like rejection if your inner voice adds, *"The sky is falling. Nothing will ever be the same."*

Let's revisit the tornado. My initial emotion was pure, unfiltered fear—a survival instinct triggered by howling winds and a house-shaking thud. But once the immediate danger passed, my feelings took over, weaving a slightly dramatic narrative.

"Love yourself first and everything else falls into line. You really have to love yourself to get anything done in this world."

- LUCILLE BALL

Assessing Your Feelings

Step 1: Reflect on your current feelings and tendencies. Some are easy to work with, while others might be challenging.

Step 2: Using the bank of feelings below, circle the common feelings you experience weekly or monthly.

Admiration   Adoration   Aesthetic Appreciation   Amusement   Anger

Anxiety   Awe   Awkwardness   Boredom   Calmness   Confusion

Craving   Curiosity   Disgust   Envy   Empathetic Pain   Entrancement

Excitement   Fear   Guilt   Horror   Interest   Joy   Jealousy   Nostalgia

Relief   Romance   Sadness   Satisfaction   Sexual Desire   Shame   Surprise

Step 3: Reflect on Your Current Status. Consider how these feelings mix together in your daily life. Are you surfing or sinking? Write down your thoughts. Think for a minute about which feelings are the most powerful and which are the most frequent.

Record your thoughts:

Riding the Emotional Current

Let's begin to distinguish between your immediate emotional reactions and the stories you attach to them. This awareness can help you respond more mindfully to life's challenges.

Step 1: Recall a recent emotional reaction. Write down the raw emotion (e.g., fear, anger, joy).

Step 2: Name the feeling. What story did your mind attach to this emotion? (e.g., "I'm overwhelmed, I can't handle this.")

Step 3: Pause and reflect.Was this story helpful or harmful? How might you rewrite the story in a supportive way? Give it a try.

THE SACRED PAUSE

The story my ego was spinning with my emotions wasn't helpful or even accurate. If I hadn't paused to separate the raw emotion from the layered feelings, I could have easily let it hijack my actions. Instead, I stopped, took a breath, and checked in with myself. That small act of awareness helped me see the emotion for what it was and let the feelings—those pesky storytellers—take a backseat.

Speaking of the "pause"—feeling overwhelmed by emotions like grief or fear is natural. Judging yourself harshly for experiencing these emotions doesn't help anyone. Take time to be with these emotions before deciding what to do next. Recognizing and honoring these experiences is key to emotional health and growth.

When you pause, you interrupt your brain's automatic stress response, giving yourself a chance to engage your higher reasoning. This pause allows you to step out of reactivity and into intention (or creativity). The pause is more than just a momentary relief—it's a habit that, over time, rewires your brain for clarity, resilience, and compassion.

Power Pause Practice

To break free from automatic reactions, try this guided pause exercise to create space between your emotions and your responses. For this exercise, set a reminder three times a day to stop and take five slow, deep breaths. Ask yourself:

What am I feeling right now?

Is this emotion asking for attention or action?

Jot down any insights that arise.

WAVE ACTION

As we learned in the 'Free Your Mind' chapter, reacting to outside circumstances and related emotions without awareness is a hallmark of reactivity. It's the autopilot mode that pulls us into old patterns. That is just one way to interact with emotions. The three most common ways people deal with emotions are **observer, avoidance, and over-identifying.** To break it down, let's try thinking of emotions as waves.

The **conscious observer** is like a beach with a natural slope and soft sand; the waves push onto the shore, crash, and recede. Pretty standard, right?

Over-identifying with emotion is like a strong undertow. When the wave starts to recede, we lose our footing and get swept into deeper waters.

Avoiding emotions is like a wave violently pounding against a sea wall, eroding away at the wall over time.

When it comes to emotional regulation, adopting the conscious observer mode is one of the healthiest strategies. This mindset allows us to acknowledge and validate our emotions without becoming overwhelmed or controlled by them. By observing our feelings with curiosity rather than judgment, we create space to respond thoughtfully instead of impulsively. For example, when we feel sadness, we can practice noticing the emotion as it arises—recognizing it without trying to suppress or overanalyze it.

It's easy to get swept up in emotions when they start to feel familiar, especially when they align with longstanding stories we tell ourselves. Emotions amplify when we turn a single feeling into a repeating narrative: *"This always happens to me." "I'll never find someone who appreciates me."* At this point, we're not just feeling loneliness but building on it, creating the fear of loneliness. Stacking stories on top of the original experience only deepens our attachment to the emotion.

Ignoring emotions is the equivalent of building a sea wall. Avoidant behavior blocks or tries to push back, but emotions don't go away when ignored. They keep coming, often with more intensity. Eventually, the suppressed emotions create cracks and erosion, breaching the seawall with force. It takes a tremendous amount of energy to maintain a wall. The energy could be used more constructively, like creating your best life.

Most of our suffering doesn't come from actual circumstances; it comes from the endless thoughts spinning in our heads, blowing up small concerns into big catastrophes. By avoiding our emotions or over-identifying with them, we create mental dis-ease and potentially physical disease. A conscious observer sees emotion as pieces of information instead of exaggerated stories or something to fear. By staying in the conscious observer mode and checking in with your emotional sensitivity levels, you can create a safe space for your emotions to come and go. The balance of compassionate witnessing and gentle redirection builds emotional resilience, helping you acknowledge your feelings without letting them hijack your reality.

Emotional Surfing

Let's explore how you currently navigate emotional waves and how you might surf them more gracefully.

Step 1: Reflect on a recent emotional situation. Circle the action that applies. Did you:

- *Observe* the emotion without judgment (calmly noticed the wave)?
- *Avoid* the emotion (blocked the wave)?
- *Over-identify* with the emotion (got pulled under by the wave)?

Step 2: How could you approach a similar emotion differently next time?

RIDING THE WAVE

Now that we've untangled feelings from emotions and dissected common ways people deal with emotions, let's add one more player to the mix: emotional intelligence (EI). If emotions are the waves and feelings are the stories about the waves, emotional intelligence is your surfboard skills. It's what keeps you from wiping out when life gets choppy.

Here's how EI ties it all together:

Recognizing the Wave: Emotional intelligence starts with awareness—spotting the emotion as it rises. You don't need to fight it or judge it. Just notice it. Is it fear? Sadness? Anger? Identifying the emotion is like spotting a wave on the horizon.

Separating Fact from Fiction: Feelings are like the overly dramatic friend who turns everything into a soap opera. EI helps you step back and ask, *"Is this true? Or is my ego adding extra spice to the story?"* This pause creates room to respond thoughtfully rather than react impulsively.

Choosing Your Response: Once you've identified and separated the emotion from the story, EI empowers you to decide what happens next. Do you ride the wave gracefully, let it crash without resistance, or steer toward calmer waters?

During the tornado cleanup, my emotions told me: *"This is overwhelming."* My feelings wanted to add: *"You'll never handle this. Just give up now."* But EI stepped in with a lifeline: *"Pause. What's one small thing you can control right now?"* That simple shift—choosing to focus on small, manageable actions—helped me stay true to my values even in the chaos.

Without emotional intelligence, you're at the mercy of the waves and the stories they create. One moment, you're scared; the next, you're spinning a tale about how life is unfair, and before you know it, you're drowning in self-doubt. But with EI, you become the surfer who rides the waves with balance and intention.

When you practice EI, you stop seeing emotions as threats and start viewing them as guides. Fear isn't here to ruin your day—it's here to protect you. Sadness isn't a sign of weakness—it's a signal to slow down and process. When you treat emotions as data and feelings as stories, you gain the power to rewrite the narrative in a way that serves you.

So, the next time life throws you a curveball—or a tornado—grab your emotional surfboard, take a breath, and ride the wave. You're stronger, smarter, and more resilient than you think.

Emotional Surfboard Toolkit

Let's build your Emotional Surfboard—a personal toolkit of strategies that help you stay balanced during emotional waves.

Step 1: Recognize the wave.What physical or mental signs tell you a strong emotion is rising?

Step 2: Stabilize the board. List two grounding techniques you can use when emotions peak (e.g., deep breathing, a mantra, stepping outside).

Step 3: Ride it out.What small, supportive action can you take to let the emotion pass without reacting impulsively?

BOTTOM LINE

So, when the winds of chaos start to howl, remember this: You've got everything you need to ride the waves. You just need a little practice. You might stumble and get a little wet, but eventually you'll find your footing and come out stronger and more in tune with yourself on the other side. It's the everyday things that will make the difference. Taking the time to identify and process your emotions is one of the smartest investments you will ever make in your self-love journey.

Love yourself like you mean it!

"We are never more fully alive, more completely ourselves, or more deeply engrossed in anything than when we are playing."

- CHARLES SCHAEFER

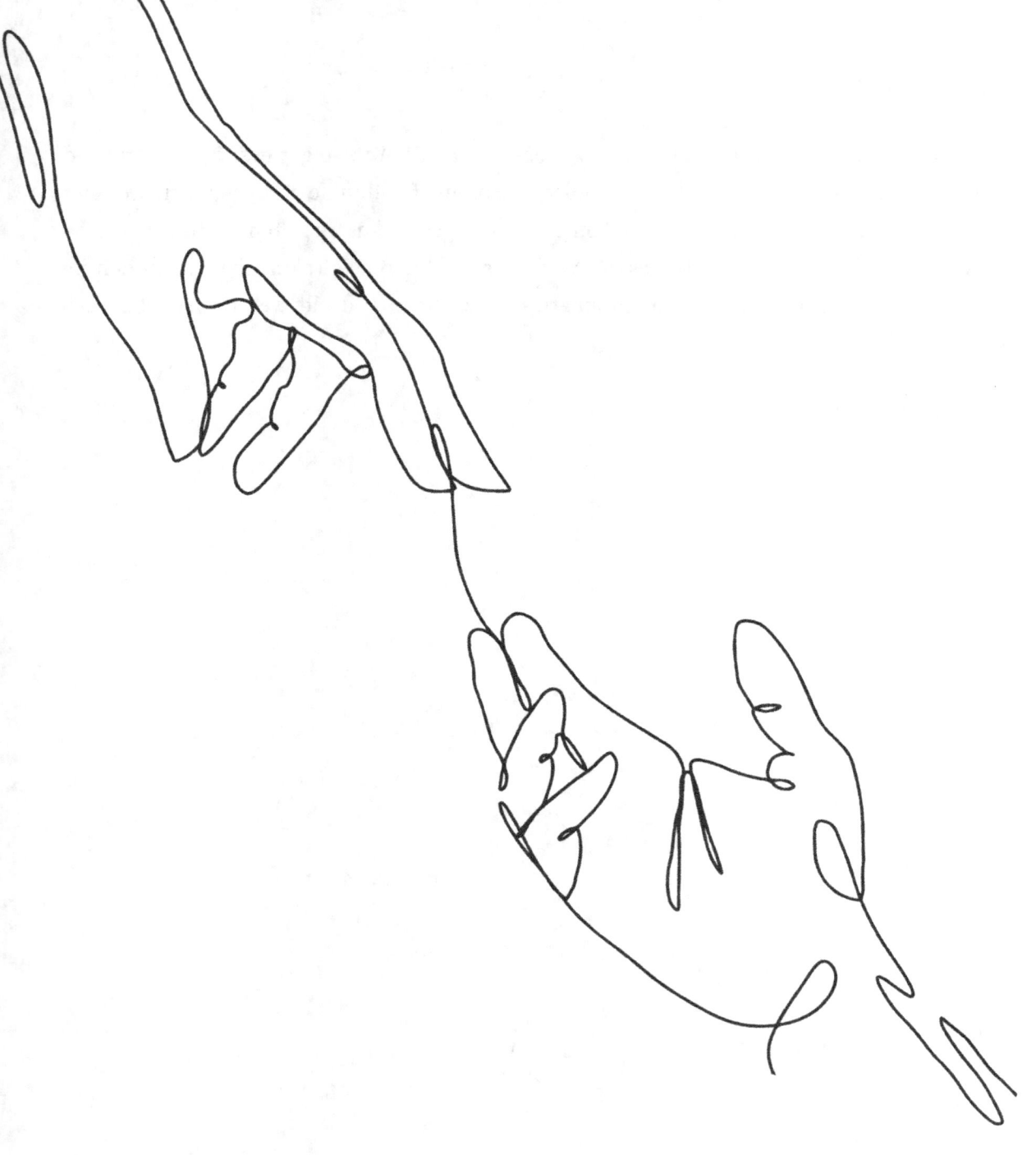

"No amount of self-improvement can make up for
any lack of self-acceptance."

- Robert Holden

08

Finding Beauty in the Brokenness

Centuries ago, a Japanese emperor broke his favorite porcelain tea bowl. Disappointed, he couldn't bear to throw it away. He sent it to be repaired, but the artisans of the time returned it to him patched with unsightly metal staples. Distraught by the poor repair job, the Emporer sent it back. Determined to find a solution worthy of the bowl's beauty, he called upon his finest craftsman to devise a better way to fix the broken dish.

What they came up with wasn't just a repair but a transformation. They used golden resin to fill the cracks, creating a piece that didn't hide its flaws but highlighted them. The once-shattered bowl was now more exquisite than ever, as each imperfection, glinting with gold, became a focal point.

This practice of repairing fine china became known as Kintsugi, which means 'golden joinery.' Over time, it evolved into an art form that celebrates beauty not in perfection but in the resilience of something that was broken and lovingly restored. The once shattered vessel transforms into something far more beautiful and valuable than the original version.

You, my friend, can transform your pieces too.

THE BREAKING POINT

As much as I admire the elegance of Kintsugi, it's hard to see the beauty when you're the one left shattered. Life has an interesting way of helping us prioritize what's important. By midlife, we often stare at a jumbled mess called our life and wonder how—and if—we'll ever put it all back together again. For me, it happened during a time when I faced an avalanche of stressors.

My husband's business took an unexpected turn, throwing our finances into chaos and forcing us to downsize and move. For six relentless months, my parents seemed to tag team short stents in the hospital about every two weeks with different health issues. Two of the most influential women in my life, my mother and my great-grandmother, passed away in the same 24 hours. As if that wasn't enough, something was always going wrong at the farm—a broken piece of equipment, animals getting out—there seemed to be a continuous list of problems to solve and fires to put out.

The real breaking point came with the kind of late-night phone call that paralyzes you with fear. The voice on the other end asked for Yavonne Butcher. "Speaking," I replied, slightly annoyed by the late-night interruption. The next words were like a punch to the gut: "Your son is in the emergency room with a stab wound to the heart. He's stable and will be admitted to the ICU."

The drive to the hospital felt like an eternity. Eventually, we got through it all. My father's health stabilized, we sold the farm, mourned my mother and great-grandmother, and my son recovered, and all seemed to go back to normal. So I thought.

I was so busy caring for everyone else that I neglected to care for myself. Spiritually disconnected, emotionally drained, and stretched far too thin in all directions, I didn't recognize myself. The toll it was taking came in the form of panic attacks from out of nowhere. That's when my doctor prescribed anti-anxiety meds—a big wake-up call for someone who doesn't even take Advil.

It wasn't just the external events that chipped away my facade of strength—it was the realization that I had been holding myself together with duct tape and denial for years. It turns out life's challenges aren't just interruptions; they're invitations. They invite us to stop, reflect, and, if we're brave enough, transform.

Identify the Broken Pieces

Step 1: Take a moment to reflect on the unresolved areas of your life that feel broken, messy, or imperfect. These could be recent challenges, past grudges and regrets, or ongoing struggles. Write down at least three in the space below.

Crack One:

Crack Two:

Crack Three:

Step 2: Explore the impact. For each situation or person listed, consider how holding onto these feelings has affected your emotional well-being, relationships, and overall happiness. Write down the specific ways clinging to this mindset has impacted your life. Think about how it has shaped you. Next, reframe the situation. Consider what you can learn from the experience. What can you be grateful for? Write down any insights, lessons, or strengths from these difficult experiences.

Crack One

- *Impact:*

- *Insight/Strength:*

Crack Two

- *Impact:*

- *Insight/Strength:*

Crack Three

- *Impact:*

- *Insight/Strength:*

Step 3: Fill the cracks with gold. Just like in the art of Kintsugi, where cracks are filled with gold to create something more beautiful, consider how you can fill the cracks in your life using gratitude and forgiveness. For each crack, write down a positive affirmation or action you can take to embrace and transform this part of your life.

- *Example:* Crack One: I lost the love of my life.
- *Affirmation:* I am grateful that a beautiful person shared their life with me.

Crack One Declaration/Action:

Crack Two Declaration/Action:

Crack Three Declaration/Action:

Step 4: Discover the lessons learned. Based on the information you've written so far, what valuable lessons did you learn from these challenging experiences? How have these lessons shaped your perspective on life?

Step 5: Embrace your unique beauty. How have these cracks contributed to the unique, one-of-a-kind person you are today? Write a short paragraph celebrating the beauty of your journey, including the cracks.

COCOON TIME

As a woman, you've likely been the glue for your family, friends, and community, holding things together no matter what. So when your life feels in pieces, the idea of slowing down to focus on your healing can feel indulgent, even selfish. If that happens, remind yourself you cannot pour from an empty cup. It is time to cocoon.

Creating a safe space where you can refuel and regenerate is essential. Give yourself permission to rest, reflect, and reconnect. Consider it an extension of the sacred pause. Just as the pause allows you to separate emotions from feelings and choose your response with intention, Cocoon Time offers the same opportunity on a larger scale. The cocoon creates a sanctuary for your mind, body, and spirit to process, repair, and ultimately emerge stronger.

We all come into this world a shiny new vessel—unmarked and full of potential. We become fractured when the ego starts to form. It takes our human experiences and, in an effort to protect us, forms judgments. The unworthy parts of ourselves get broken off and banished to the shadow side, hidden but never gone.

Over time, these judgments and life's inevitable hardships—loss, rejection, or trauma combine to create more fractures inside us. A marriage that falls apart, a career that derails, or the heartbreak of losing someone we love—each event highlights the broken pieces more and more. These pieces are your call to create something new. They are an opportunity to examine, heal, and transform. Healing requires offering yourself the same compassion you so generously extend to others. Like the process of Kintsugi, healing is deliberate and patient, reconnecting step by step. It begins with acknowledging your brokenness—laying out the pieces of your pain and experiences to see them clearly.

Next comes reflection, the tool to assess your inner world with care and intention so rebuilding can take place. Just as broken fragments must be cleaned and prepared, healing asks you to confront and smooth out the emotional residue that holds you back. Over time, with love, patience, and persistence, you begin to reconnect the pieces. By holding space for the process to unfold, you allow forgiveness, vulnerability, and gratitude to create a lasting bond.

ESSENTIAL ELEMENTS OF THE HEALING PROCESS

In a Kintsugi project, you must clean and prepare the shards, apply sticky tree resin, and finally dust the cracks with gold powder to piece the vessel together. We also require three essential elements; forgiveness, vulnerability, and gratitude.

Forgiveness prepares the way for transformation. It cleans and smooths the fractured edges, removing the emotional residue that keeps us stuck. Just as preparation ensures the lacquer will bond the pottery, forgiveness softens us, making space for peace and lasting repair.

Vulnerability is the courageous act of acknowledging our brokenness, just as sticky tree resin binds the pieces of shattered pottery back together. Without vulnerability, the healing process cannot begin.

Gratitude highlights the cracks. Like the gold in Kintsugi, gratitude highlights the beauty and value in our scars, helping us see the growth and strength that emerge from difficult experiences. It's what makes the repair more extraordinary than before.

Each element plays a unique role in the healing process. Together, these emotional experiences form the trinity of transformation, taking us from brokenness to wholeness. Let's explore how each element works together to help us heal, grow, and shine.

Loving Yourself Through the Brokenness

Step 1: Develop strategies to love yourself through the challenges of life. By practicing self-love, you'll continue to repair those cracks with gold. How can you love yourself during difficult times? List three loving actions you can take when feeling overwhelmed or broken.

Your Self-Love Plan:

Step 2: Practice gratitude and forgiveness. Reflect on one challenge you're currently facing or have recently overcome.

What is one thing you're grateful for in this experience?

Is there someone you need to forgive (consider yourself)?

How can you express gratitude for the growth this challenge is bringing you?

LETTING GO

Forgiveness is the yellow brick road that leads you home. It's the process of releasing resentment and anger to make space for love to flourish.

Letting go doesn't mean erasing the past or giving a free pass to those who've hurt you. It allows you to reclaim the energy tied up in old wounds and repurpose it to create the life you crave.

Each act of forgiveness turns a raw, jagged wound into a line of brilliance, a testament to your ability to alchemize pain into power. Our pain is often rooted in the frustration of unmet expectations or the sting of perceived injustices. We imagine how things should have gone or hold onto the belief that someone else should take responsibility for our hurt. This attachment to how others act or should have acted can create a sense of powerlessness because, in truth, we can never control someone else's choices or behavior. Forgiveness invites us to release that futile attempt at control and reclaim power over our outer world.

When someone hurts us, it's natural to wish we could make them understand the depth of our pain, apologize, or change their ways. This desire for control is understandable, but it often leads to prolonged suffering. As long as we hinge our emotional peace on someone else's actions, we remain stuck, tethered to a cycle of frustration and disappointment.

Forgiveness is the act of stepping off the merry-go-round of blame and resentment, freeing yourself from the exhausting cycle of rehearsing hurt and fantasizing about revenge. It doesn't mean condoning harmful behavior or pretending it didn't happen—it's about reclaiming your peace by shifting the focus inward. Forgiveness invites you to let go of the need to win or get even, not to let someone off the hook but to choose yourself. Holding onto anger can feel like self-protection, yet it often hurts more than the original wound. By releasing what no longer serves you, forgiveness helps you regain control over your emotional state, allowing you to feel liberated, peaceful, and unburdened by the past.

When you let go of the need to control outcomes or others, you open up space for clarity. This clarity allows you to evaluate relationships more thoughtfully, set boundaries where needed, and decide what role (if any) the person who hurt you will play in your life moving forward.

Letting go of control through forgiveness isn't about giving up—it's about stepping into your own power. By choosing peace and prioritizing your emotional well-being, you liberate yourself from the chains of resentment and step into a life defined not by what happened to you but by how you chose to respond.

A Letter of Forgiveness

Think of a person or situation you have difficulty forgiving. On a separate paper, scribe a letter to the person you need to forgive (this can be you or someone else). Be sure to address the pain and acknowledge the impact. Don't hold back. Let it all out on the page. Then, if you are ready to see the situation from their perspective, express empathy and understanding, then forgive them. Close the letter with gratitude.

Take your time writing the letter. Do not censor yourself; fill as many pages as you'd like. When you're done, decide what to do with the letter. You can keep it as a reminder of your journey, destroy it as a symbol of release, or, if appropriate, share it with the other person.

THE COURAGE TO BE SEEN

Vulnerability is often misunderstood as a weakness—a crack in the armor that leaves us exposed. In reality, it is the most courageous act we can embrace. Vulnerability is the willingness to lay down the mask, strip away the pretense, and show up authentically. It's stepping into the world without guarantees, opening yourself up to both joy and pain, darkness and light.

When you embrace vulnerability, you break the cycle of hiding the parts of yourself judged unworthy. The cracks in your armor, the ones you've spent so much time patching and hiding, are actually the gateways to connection and transformation. You unlock the door to healing when you allow yourself to be seen.

Vulnerability breaks the silence. The stories we keep locked inside—the ones about shame, failure, or fear—lose their power when they are brought into the light. Naming your pain, whether to yourself or a trusted person, is an act of release. It's saying, *"This is what I'm carrying, but it doesn't define me."*

Vulnerability facilitates connection. We often think our exposed cracks will alienate us, but the opposite is true. When you share your struggles, you create a bridge for others to meet you where you are.

In the quiet moments of sitting with your pain, you may feel the urge to avoid it, to distract yourself, or to deny it altogether. Vulnerability asks you to do the opposite. It asks you to lean in, sit with the discomfort, and trust yourself. The person who emerges from this process will be stronger, more beautiful, and whole.

The parts of yourself you feared would be judged or rejected become the very things that connect you to others and to your deeper self. The paradox of vulnerability is that you discover your inner strength and hidden talents by allowing yourself to be seen. Vulnerability honors the cracks. It transforms them into spaces where love can take root and where healing begins.

"With every prayer, every thought of forgiveness, every meditation, every act of love, we plug in."

- MARIANNE WILLIAMSON

Self-Worth in Connections

This exercise aims to understand how relationships can reflect unresolved areas of self-worth and cultivate self-compassion through this awareness. This exercise helps you understand that what feels like external conflict is often an invitation for internal healing.

Step 1: Think of a recent conflict or situation in a close relationship where you felt particularly insecure, hurt, or triggered. Write it down.

Step 2: Ask yourself:

- "What part of me felt attacked at this moment?"
- "How does this situation mirror my beliefs about my self-worth?"

Step 3: Practice self-compassion. Using the insights from Step 2, write a compassionate letter to yourself. Acknowledge that insecurity is understandable and human, but remind yourself that this external situation doesn't define your value. Offer yourself love and kindness as if comforting a dear friend or a small child.

Dear _____,

When you feel broken, lack often becomes the loudest voice in the room. Rooted in moments where love, stability, or protection feel absent, this voice speaks lies. It lays the foundation for illusions. It convinces you that your worth is tied to what's missing, driving you to seek external security instead of trusting the wholeness already inside you.

Gratitude doesn't just change how you view your circumstances; it changes how you see yourself. It encourages you to look beyond what's missing and recognize what's still there. When you begin to appreciate the small, overlooked aspects of your life, you start to notice the things about yourself worth celebrating: your persistence, creativity, and ability to get up and keep going, even when life feels impossibly hard. Gratitude doesn't just mean acknowledging the beauty around you—it means uncovering the treasure within you.

Take my story, for example. After a few years of relentless stress, I finally hit my breaking point. Anxiety had become my constant companion, and I found myself numb and disconnected. One day, three weeks into a new prescription, I stood at the kitchen sink, humming a tune while washing dishes (something I used to do all the time). It was a simple act, but it hit me like lightning: I hadn't felt like myself in years. That small, ordinary moment sparked a flicker of gratitude. It reminded me I wasn't truly lost. I just needed help finding my way back.

That realization marked the beginning of my healing journey. I stopped viewing my brokenness as proof of failure and started asking questions that nurtured growth: *"What am I learning? What have I been neglecting? What is this moment trying to show me?"* These questions were like golden threads, weaving meaning and resilience into my life.

Gratitude doesn't just plaster over the cracks; it reframes them. Like the gold in Kintsugi, it shifts your focus from what's broken to what's beautiful, from what's gone wrong to what's still good. Each acknowledgment of gratitude adds to the golden glow of your story, illuminating the resilience and abundance already present inside you.

Gratitude, when practiced over time, becomes transformative. It rewires your mindset, teaching you to seek joy and meaning even in difficulty. It stops the comparison cycle and helps you see that your value doesn't come from perfection or external validation. Instead of erasing the memory, it reminds you that you are not defined by what happened. Your worth lies in your ability to find beauty in the brokenness and new meaning in the cracks.

So, the next time life feels shattered, take a moment to pause. Look at the pieces, the cracks, and the jagged edges. Ask yourself, *"What can I be grateful for right now?"* It might be something small, like the warmth of sunlight on your face, or something profound, like the unwavering support of a friend. Whatever it is, let it anchor you.

Focusing on forgiveness, gratitude, and vulnerability during your cocoon phase is a level of healing that requires courage. It's not always pretty, but it's the only path to wholeness because it strips away the ego's illusions and shines a light of love into the subconscious. It reconnects you to your soul—the self that has always been whole, even when life tries to convince you otherwise.

Mindful Gratitude Practice

Choose one mundane task you do regularly, such as folding laundry, washing dishes, or preparing meals. The next time you perform this task, do it mindfully. Focus on each action, and as you do, think about the people in your life who benefit from your efforts (including you). Write down your reflections after a week of practicing mindfulness during your chosen task.

Pro Tip: If you need help getting your mind in the present, check in with your five senses.

Task Chosen: _____

Reflection Questions:

- How did focusing on gratitude change your experience of the task?

- What emotions did you feel during this practice?

- How can you incorporate this mindful gratitude into other areas of your life?

Golden Thread Reflection

This exercise helps you trace the "golden threads" of wisdom and growth that emerged from painful experiences.

Step 1: Reflect on a past struggle that deeply impacted you. What lessons or strengths have you gained from this experience?

Step 2: Draw a broken object (a heart, a bowl, or whatever you want to draw).

Step 3: In each crack of the image you drew, write the lessons, insights, or strengths you gained.

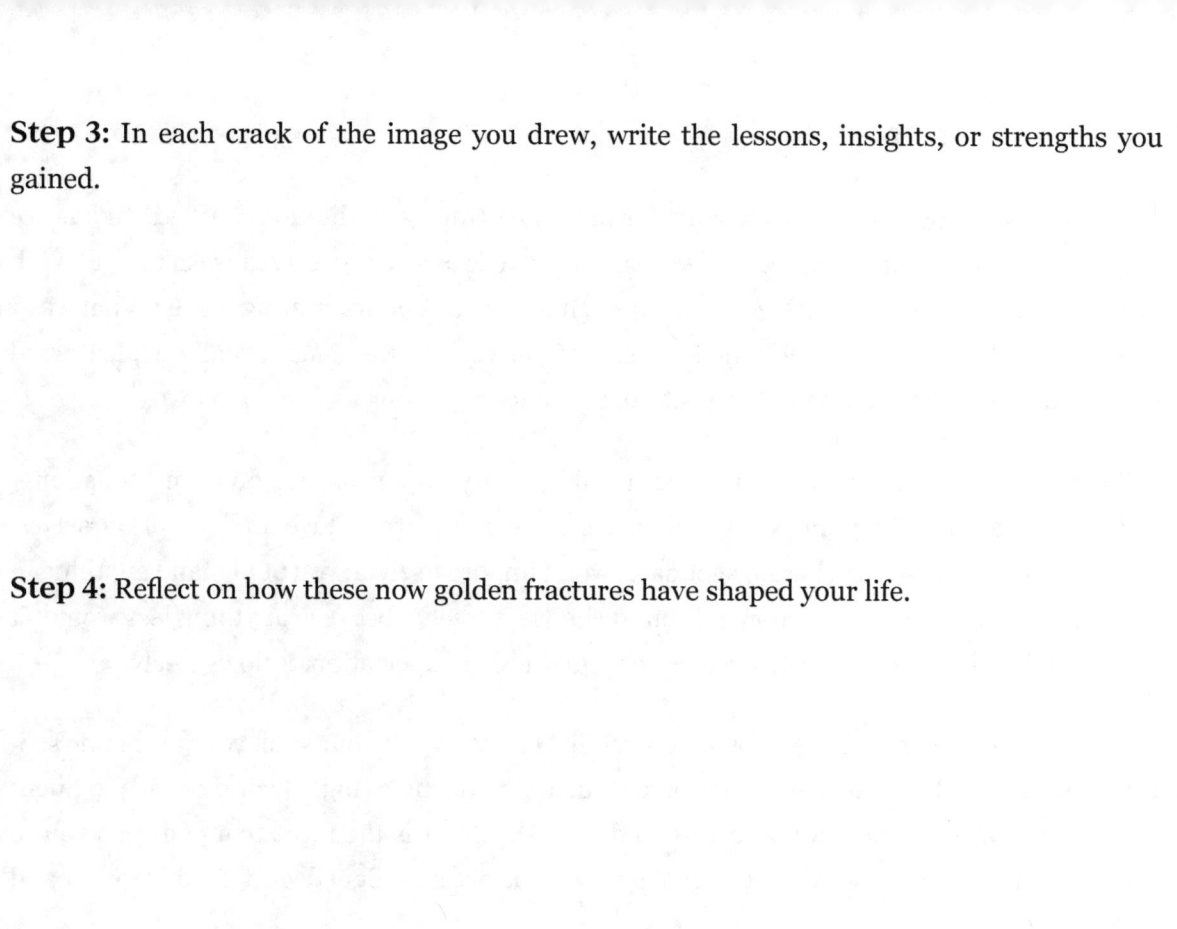

Step 4: Reflect on how these now golden fractures have shaped your life.

THE FINAL MASTERPIECE

Years ago, in my twenties, I was looking for direction. During meditation, I asked, *"What are my talents? What occupation do I need to pursue?"* The answer I received wasn't about a job or a skill set. It was simply *'LOVE.'* At the time, it felt vague and frustrating. Love? What was I supposed to do with that? Each time I asked, the answer was the same. Eventually, I stopped asking and decided it didn't matter what I did for a living as long as I acted in love.

I didn't realize until much later that I'd missed one very important person in my equation—MYSELF! We cannot genuinely love others until we first learn to love and accept ourselves. True love in its purest form has no agenda. It won't impose itself on you or demand anything in return. Love patiently waits, allowing you to choose it freely—because anything less wouldn't be love. When you decide to BE love, without pressure or expectation, it flows freely.

Unconditional love isn't just an abstract idea—it's the energy of your soul, your authentic self. It resonates from the deepest part of you, untouched by the noise of the world or the judgment of your ego. This love is pure, limitless, and unshakable. It is the force that connects you to something far greater than yourself. That's why if you are not aligned with it, you crave it and look for it everywhere!

Love is the great liberator. In the words of the Mind Architect Peter Crone, *"Life will present you with people and circumstances to reveal where you are not free."* When the "I," that is, the ego, surrenders to unconditional love, we experience freedom. Freedom from the illusions of lack, fear, and separation. It doesn't demand perfection. Love whispers that you are enough exactly as you are. It doesn't require you to fix yourself before you're worthy.

Love is a boundless resource without walls. Unlike material possessions, love doesn't diminish when shared—it multiplies, creating a ripple effect of connection and joy. Love is not finite; it's an ever-expanding force that flourishes with generosity. When you care and love yourself, you maintain the capacity to love others. The more love you give, the more you cultivate the more it returns to you. By extending care, kindness, and compassion to others, you tap into an abundant wellspring of love that nourishes both the giver and the receiver. Love thrives on connection, proving that we are also receiving in the act of giving—a powerful reminder that true love knows no limits.

What if the purpose of life is to simply enjoy it? Love flourishes in an atmosphere of joy and playfulness, where laughter and lightheartedness nurture self-connection and inner peace. Maintaining your child-like capacity for curiosity is a breeding ground for self-love. When you take life too seriously, you risk stifling your ability to love fully, turning self-care into a task rather than a celebration of who you are. Joy invites us to release our defenses, embrace our authentic selves, and find delight in our individuality.

At its core, love is the meaning of life. It gives us direction and depth in our existence. It's not just something we feel or share but the very essence of why we are here. Your body knows the difference between love and fear. It is sending you signals all the time. By making love the foundation, we inadvertently create a legacy that ripples far beyond our individual lives, touching others with kindness, connection, and understanding. In the end, to live centered in love is to live a life of true fulfillment and profound impact.

"How much we know and understand ourselves is critically important, but there is something that is even more essential in living a wholehearted life: loving ourselves."

- BRENE BROWN

Connecting to The Heart of Me

This exercise aims to create a visual representation of the love within yourself, helping you connect with feelings of self-compassion, worthiness, and joy.

Materials Needed:

- Colored pencils, markers, or crayons
- Optional: magazines for collage, glue, scissors

Step 1: Prepare Your Space. Find a quiet and comfortable place where you can focus without distractions. Set an intention for this activity, such as "I want to connect with the love inside me."

Step 2: Close your eyes for a moment and take a few deep breaths. Imagine a warm light glowing in your chest, representing the love within you. How does it feel? What colors, shapes, or images come to mind when you think of this inner love? Get curious and take as much time as you need to do this step.

Step 3: Create Your Heart. In the space provided, draw a large heart in the center to symbolize your inner love. Within or around this heart, use colors, patterns, symbols, or images that represent how love feels to you. Leave enough space around the heart to do step 4.

Step 4: Around the heart, draw or write elements of your life where this love flows outward. Think about relationships, activities, or qualities you cherish. Let your design flow naturally.

Step 5: Reflect on the Art. Once you've completed your piece, take a moment to sit with it. Observe the colors, patterns, and feelings that come up as you look at your work.

How does this artwork reflect the love inside you?

Did any unexpected feelings, symbols, or insights emerge during this process?

What part of your design feels most meaningful or alive? Why?

How can this representation of love inspire or guide you in your daily life?

Brainstorm some ways you can grow this love further.

THE SOUL FEELS ITS WORTH

Have you ever felt your true worth? I'm not talking about knowing your worth—that's different. I'm talking about the combination of knowing and feeling your worth at the same time. It happened to me during one of my many meditations, and I've never forgotten it.

When you are in the moment, when your soul feels its worth, no human words can truly describe it. It does not come from a cause and effect outside of us; it is something that radiates from the inside out. The only words I can think of that come close to describing it is a wholeness born from unconditional love—the feeling of total acceptance where nothing and no one is more or less than: there is no judgment, no hoops to jump through; you are perfectly complete.

When the soul feels its worth, your perception changes. You feel connected to yourself and all of creation at the same time. The realization of the vastness that is love humbles you. You feel tiny but not insignificant. You sit in stillness and radiate a quiet peace—a rock-solid confidence. From this foundation rises a knowing of your purpose followed by the feeling of joy and then profound humility. You experience a deep gratitude for all the things, good or bad, painful or joyful, that got you where you are right now.

After experiencing this moment, nothing is worth holding on to except that feeling. It makes it easier to let go of everything we thought was important. Not only that, but the blinders come off, and you really see the world. Your body feels lighter, and colors appear more vivid. You feel transformed.

Love holds a neutral space—a judgment-free zone—for you to feel and know the beauty and true power of your fullness. What are you waiting for?

"Aging seems to be the only
available way to live a long life."

- KITTY O'NEILL COLLINS

Nurture The Inner Child

Incorporate small, daily practices that nurture the love and playfulness of your inner child, bringing lightness and connection into your everyday life. Repeat this practice daily or as often as you can. Over time, you'll strengthen your connection to playfulness and love, creating a habit of finding lightness in everyday moments. This simple commitment is a gift to yourself—a reminder that joy is always within reach.

Step 1: Set a Daily Joy Reminder. Choose one simple, playful activity that resonates with your inner child each morning. This could be anything that feels light, joyful, or whimsical—something you loved as a child or something that delights you today.

Step 2: Anchor It in Your Day. Pair this activity with something you already do daily, such as making coffee, brushing your teeth, or taking a break at work. Let the activity be a moment to reconnect with joy and playfulness, no matter how small.

Examples:

- Blow bubbles while enjoying a glass of wine in your backyard.
- Draw or doodle when you're sitting in a waiting room or airport.
- Skip as you leave the house for work. Sing your favorite childhood song in the shower.
- Watch the clouds and find shapes or star gaze for a few minutes while in your yard.

Step 3: Be present in the moment. While doing the activity, pause to fully immerse yourself. Notice how playing, laughing, or creating without judgment or a goal feels. Let yourself experience the carefree wonder of your inner child.

Step 4: At the end of the day, reflect on your playful moments. In your journal, write down a sentence or two about how it feels to embrace your inner child. If it brought a smile, warmth, or energy, acknowledge it and give yourself gratitude for prioritizing the love and joy inside you.

Time to Celebrate

Reflect on your transformation. Take time to reflect on changes in how you perceive your life and yourself. Use the space below to write about your experience.

What changes have you noticed in your self-perception after consistently practicing forgiveness, vulnerability, and gratitude?

How has embracing brokenness changed your outlook on life?

What positive changes have you noticed in your self-perception?

How can you continue to apply the principles of Kintsugi to your life moving forward?

BOTTOM LINE

Life often mirrors the art of Kintsugi. We come into this world as pristine shiny new vessels, equipped to flourish. Over time, the ego creates fractures in our inner world. These cracks are not the end of our story but an invitation to transform.

We begin to piece ourselves back together through forgiveness, vulnerability, and gratitude. Each act of healing fills the fractures with the gold of self-compassion, resilience, and wisdom. The vessel that emerges is not the same as it once was; it is something entirely different—more valuable, more beautiful, and far more interesting because of the journey it endured.

This final masterpiece reflects the transformative power of love. Love is the force that unites us with our soul. Love doesn't erase the cracks; it celebrates them, showing us that they are what make us extraordinary.

When we choose love, we no longer see ourselves as broken but as beautifully whole, transformed by the process of being human. The masterpiece we become is a testament to love, a unique reflection of our authenticity.

Love whispers, "Come home."

Conclusion

FULLY FLOURISH BY LOVING FIERCELY

So here we are at the end of this book—or maybe it's better to think of it as the beginning of something new. If you take away just one thing, let it be this: *You already have everything you need inside you to flourish.* You don't need fixing, improving, or reinventing. You are not an unfinished project. **You're a masterpiece—surrender to that fact!**

Over the past chapters, we've explored what it means to flourish—not by chasing perfection or someone else's version of success, but by uncovering the beauty, strength, and wisdom deep inside you all along. We've talked about peeling back the ego, setting boundaries, and embracing our humanness. Together, we've seen how real, unconditional love can transform life's messes into meaning.

Flourishing isn't about eliminating challenges, smoothing out every wrinkle, or finally figuring out the secret formula for never making mistakes again. Flourishing is about showing up—fully, authentically, unapologetically as YOU. It's about letting love be the loudest voice in your head.

And yes, it's about embracing the messy parts, too. Life will always be full of surprises—big ones, little ones, good ones, bad ones, and the occasional Nerf dart when you least expect it. The goal isn't to avoid the chaos but to dance through it. To laugh, to stumble, to cry if you need to, and to remember that every step forward—no matter how wobbly—is still progress.

THE STEPS TO FLOURISHING

Flourishing is a lifestyle, a series of small, intentional choices made every day. This book has offered tools to help you navigate the journey:

Reconnect with Your Inner Compass: Your core values are your GPS. By aligning your life with these profoundly personal truths, you create a foundation for authenticity and fulfillment. Shedding fear-based beliefs and societal expectations frees you from the need for external validation, allowing you to set healthy boundaries and make choices rooted in love, not fear. This alignment with your soul's purpose empowers you to live a life of intention, creativity, and joy.

Free Your Mind: Limiting beliefs from childhood act as an invisible prison, keeping you stuck in fear and self-doubt. By understanding the roots of these patterns and reframing them, you can break free from reactivity and step into your power as the creator of your life. This shift from ego-driven scarcity to soul-guided abundance allows you to approach life with clarity, confidence, and purpose.

Embrace the Brokenness: Life's cracks are not flaws but invitations to transform. Just as Kintsugi repairs broken pottery with gold, turning it into something even more beautiful, you can use forgiveness, vulnerability, and gratitude to heal and grow. By honoring your scars and seeing the strength in your resilience, you can turn setbacks into golden seams of wisdom, creating a masterpiece from your experiences.

Live From Unconditional Love: The love you seek has always been within you. By breaking free from the ego's fear of lack, you can step into the limitless abundance of the soul. From this place of wholeness, you stop reacting to life and start living intentionally, guided by connection, creativity, and a deep trust in your inherent worth.

Flourishing means more than just surviving—it means thriving in a way that feels true to you. By choosing to live from love, authenticity, and abundance, you create a life filled with joy, peace, and purpose.

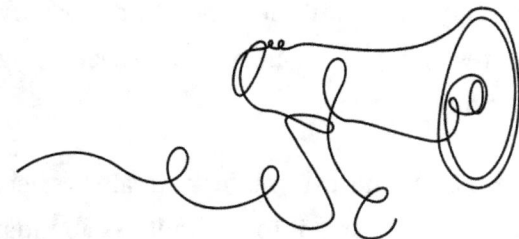

"Unconditional self-love is all about seeing yourself
as whole and complete, just as you are."

- Yung Pueblo

Your Voice Matters!

If you found value in this workbook and it helped you uncover your worth and love yourself more than ever, I'd love to hear about it! Your review doesn't just help me—it helps other women discover this resource, too. Together, we can create a movement where more women identify with their values, embrace their authenticity, and unapologetically flourish as they age.

So, if this book resonates with you, please share your thoughts by leaving a review. Your voice has the power to inspire others, and who knows? You might be the reason someone else starts their own self-love journey.

Let's start a ripple effect of self-love, strength, and joy. Together, we can make "flourishing after fifty" the new normal. Thank you for being part of this movement—you're already making a difference!

Deep Dive Resource Guide

Self-love and personal growth aren't one-size-fits-all journeys. Sometimes, we need a little extra support or a fresh perspective to navigate our paths and unlock our fullest potential. The following resources are books, tools, videos, programs, and guides I've personally explored and found valuable along my self-love journey. From uncovering core values to rewiring your mindset, these resources offer practical solutions and inspiration to deepen the transformative work you've started here.

Here are some books with valuable information:

Productivity Habits

Miracle Morning, by Hal Elrod

This book is an excellent resource for introducing a transformative morning routine designed to help you maximize your potential through practices like meditation, affirmations, and journaling. It provides a structured yet flexible framework to prioritize personal growth, self-care, and intentional living. The author created a community to support the process.

Vulnerability

Braving the Wild, by Dr. Brene Brown

In her studies, Dr. Brown explores the courage it takes to embrace vulnerability, stand in your truth, and find belonging within yourself. For women on a self-love journey, this book offers powerful lessons on building resilience, setting boundaries, and cultivating authentic connections. Brené's wisdom inspires readers to trust their inner strength and navigate life with bravery and self-compassion.

Self-Acceptance

A Course in Miracles, by Dr. Helen Schucman

This book comes with a built-in workbook. The text teaches forgiveness, self-awareness, and a path to inner peace. It offers profound insights into releasing self-judgment, overcoming fear, and recognizing one's inherent worth. By shifting perceptions from fear to love, ACIM can help readers cultivate a deeper connection with themselves and embrace their authentic inner light.

Emotional Regulation

Emotional Intelligence, by Daniel Goleman

Emotions play a critical role in our personal and relational success. The book highlights skills like self-awareness, empathy, and emotional regulation. It offers practical insights into understanding and managing emotions, fostering deeper connections, and building resilience. By strengthening emotional intelligence, readers can develop a greater sense of inner harmony and confidence in navigating life's challenges.

Core Values

The Values Factor, by Dr. John DeMartini

Dr. Demartini offers a powerful framework for aligning your life with your highest values to unlock purpose, fulfillment, and success. By identifying what matters most to you, the book helps you prioritize decisions and actions that resonate with your authentic self. For women on a self-love journey, it provides tools to cultivate clarity, self-worth, and a significant life.

Mindfulness

Joy on Demand, by Chade Meng-Tan

Chade Meng-Tan offers practical and accessible techniques for cultivating happiness and mindfulness in everyday life. It provides tools to tap into joy from within, even during challenging moments, by using simple mindfulness practices. This book helps readers strengthen their connection to inner peace and delight, making self-love a natural and effortless part of daily life.

Meditation

The 6 Phase Meditation Method, by Vishen Lakhiani

This book provides a practical, step-by-step approach to meditation that enhances mental clarity, emotional well-being, and personal transformation. It offers a powerful framework to nurture gratitude, self-compassion, and a vision for their best life. By integrating these six phases into daily practice, readers can deepen their connection to themselves and create a life rooted in love and fulfillment.

Boundaries

Boundary Boss, by Terri Cole

Boundary Boss is a transformative guide for women to recognize, set, and maintain healthy boundaries in all areas of life. It empowers readers to identify patterns of overgiving, people-pleasing, and self-neglect while teaching practical tools to communicate needs with confidence and compassion. By embracing the strategies in this book, women can create space for self-love, authenticity, and deeper, more fulfilling relationships.

Other Resources: I invite you to explore these opportunities—they just might be the key to your next breakthrough!

Lisa Pulliam Life Coach

Lisa Carol Pulliam is a transformational life coach dedicated to empowering midlife women to rediscover their purpose and thrive in the second half of life. Through her Thrive Sisterhood community and Thrive in '25 workshops, she offers personalized coaching, supportive communities, and transformative retreats designed to help women embrace their authentic selves and live with intention, courage, and confidence. Lisa's compassionate approach and commitment to personal growth make her an invaluable resource for women seeking transformation and fulfillment in midlife.

Mindvalley

Mindvalley is a comprehensive personal growth platform offering over 100 programs designed to enhance various aspects of life, including mind, body, soul, career, entrepreneurship, and relationships. Their unique 'Quest' learning approach provides structured, daily micro-coaching sessions led by world-class experts, making personal development both accessible and engaging. Mindvalley fosters a vibrant community of like-minded individuals, offering support and encouragement throughout your transformative journey. By focusing on holistic growth, Mindvalley empowers you to unlock your full potential and lead an extraordinary life.

Rewired, by Dr. Joe Dispenza

The docuseries explores the science of neuroplasticity and how changing your thoughts can transform your life. It provides actionable insights into breaking free from limiting beliefs, reprogramming the mind for positivity, and creating a new emotional and mental reality. By aligning thoughts, emotions, and intentions, viewers can cultivate deeper self-love and step into their fullest potential.

Your Mind Aligned, Kristen Burkholder

A personal development approach that integrates mindfulness, neuroscience, and intentional practices to align thoughts, emotions, and behaviors with desired outcomes. Focusing on clarity, emotional regulation, and positive visualization helps individuals shift from limiting beliefs to empowering mindsets. Align the Mind supports emotional balance, mental focus, and resilience through practical techniques like affirmations, mindfulness exercises, and goal-setting. This holistic approach encourages individuals to create a harmonious inner state that fosters self-love, personal growth, and the achievement of meaningful goals.

The Breakthrough Experience, by Dr. John Demartini

A transformative resource for anyone looking to uncover their core values and create a life of alignment and purpose. As a human behavior expert, Dr. Demartini combines psychology, philosophy, and universal principles to help individuals turn challenges into opportunities for growth. His teachings are supported by practical tools, such as the Demartini Method, designed to dissolve emotional baggage, release resentment, and cultivate gratitude and inner peace. For those seeking deeper self-awareness, empowerment, and self-love, Dr. Demartini offers a variety of resources, including a core values assessment, workshops, online courses, and personalized strategies to balance perceptions and live authentically. Whether through his book or immersive programs, The Breakthrough Experience serves as a comprehensive guide to embracing your highest potential.

BetterHelp, Get Started

A widely recognized online platform that connects individuals with licensed therapists, making mental health support more accessible and convenient. Through video calls, phone sessions, or messaging, users can receive professional counseling tailored to their specific needs, all from their homes. BetterHelp offers support for a range of concerns, including anxiety, depression, relationship challenges, and personal growth. With flexible scheduling, a diverse network of therapists, and affordable options compared to traditional therapy, BetterHelp provides a valuable resource for those seeking guidance and emotional well-being.

VARIOUS THERAPIES

Though the list is not comprehensive, the following are therapies I discovered along the way but never tried myself. According to various studies, they have been very successful in helping individuals grow to their fullest potential.

Cognitive Behavioral Therapy (CBT) and other behavioral therapies are evidence-based approaches that help individuals identify and change unhelpful thoughts and behaviors. By challenging negative thinking patterns and adopting healthier responses, these therapies empower people to manage emotions, reduce stress, and enhance well-being. They are particularly effective for overcoming anxiety, depression, and self-doubt, making them powerful tools on a self-love journey.

Dialectical Behavior Therapy (DBT) is a highly effective, evidence-based psychotherapy designed to help individuals manage intense emotions, build healthier relationships, and develop mindfulness skills. Initially created to treat borderline personality disorder, DBT has proven effective for a wide range of challenges, including anxiety, depression, and emotional dysregulation. DBT combines cognitive-behavioral techniques with mindfulness practices, emphasizing the balance between acceptance and change. Key components include learning to tolerate distress, regulate emotions, improve interpersonal effectiveness, and practice mindful awareness. DBT empowers individuals to navigate life's challenges with greater resilience and emotional balance by providing practical tools and fostering self-compassion.

Tapping, or Emotional Freedom Technique (EFT) is a powerful stress-relief method that involves gently tapping on specific acupressure points while focusing on an emotional challenge. By combining physical touch with mindful acknowledgment of feelings, tapping helps reduce stress, release negative emotions, and promote a sense of calm. It's an accessible tool for regulating emotions, improving self-awareness, and fostering self-love.

Mindfulness-Based Stress Reduction (MBSR) is an evidence-based program developed by Dr. Jon Kabat-Zinn to help individuals manage stress, anxiety, chronic pain, and other challenges through mindfulness practices. This eight-week program combines meditation, body awareness, and gentle yoga to cultivate present-moment awareness and reduce reactivity to stressors. MBSR encourages participants to approach life's difficulties with greater acceptance and curiosity, fostering emotional resilience and mental clarity. By integrating mindfulness into daily life, MBSR has improved well-being, enhanced emotional regulation, and promoted a deeper sense of peace and balance.

Citations

- TED. (2023, September 14). *The single most important parenting strategy | Becky Kennedy TED* [Video]. YouTube. *The Single Most Important Parenting Strategy | Becky Kennedy | TED*

- Dispenza, J. [drjoedispenza.com]. (2023, January 25). *Rewired* [Video]. gaia.com. Retrieved December 10, 2024, from https://www.gaia.com/series/rewired

- Clear, J. (2018). *Atomic Habits Summary (by James Clear): Summary and Illustration.* James Clear.

Let Me Introduce Myself

Hey there! I'm Yavonne Butcher—a lifelong student of human potential and a fun-loving, introspective, adventurous soul navigating life's next chapter. In this empty nesting phase of life, my days are filled with quiet morning coffee chats with my husband, long walks in nature with my loyal pup, and the occasional spontaneous dance party in the kitchen (because life is too short not to have a little fun!).

Through writing and speaking, I pursue my passion for encouraging, empowering, and inspiring people to live from a place of wholeness and peace. Flourish After Fifty explores personal growth by facilitating intersections between science and spirituality, psychology and soul. Through self-awareness, intentional living, and a shift in perception, I believe we can all move beyond survival mode and experience life with clarity, purpose, and profound joy. After all, midlife doesn't need to be a crisis—it's the perfect opportunity to rediscover yourself, break free from old limitations, and step into the fullest version of yourself by challenging old paradigms, expanding conscious awareness, and igniting transformation.

So, grab a cup of coffee (or a glass of wine), get cozy, and let's embark on this adventure together. Midlife is just the beginning—let's flourish!